"Alex is a brilliant, hilarious thinker! In this book, he **opens the door to transformational thinking** and getting outside of our own little boxes into a large vision of life and powerful living. **Wherever Alex leads, it's a good idea to follow!"**

- **Christopher McAuliffe**, *Master Certified Coach and Founder and CEO of Accomplishment Coaching*

"Alex brings a combination of **boldness, truth, and heart that's undeniable.** He truly cares, and wants to make those around him better. The feeling is contagious!"

- **Peter Guzzardi**, *author of Emeralds of Oz and editor of books by Deepak Chopra and Stephen Hawking*

"Alex Terranova has a **unique gift to create a powerful yet safe space for transformation** and growth..."

- **Dr. Erin Fall Haskell**, *best selling author of Awakening, Global Peace Leader, Founder TV Host of Good Morning LaLa Land and Soulciete*

"I met Alex early in his career and it was instantly clear to me that he has what it takes to be successful. **He's an awe-inspiring person** and it makes me very happy to know that he's sharing his talents in a way that helps others."

- **David L. Hoyt**, *"The Man Who Puzzles America" and the most syndicated puzzle maker in America*

"Alex is ferocious in his commitment to the transformation of others, and is courageous enough to be equally ferocious about his own. His wo   f personal growth is **full of heart and at the same time, honors forward movement** in the endeavors he and the people around him are taking on. Alex manages to do all this and share his voice as a leader in the world with integrity and honor along the way."

- **Mark Hunter**, *Master Certified Coach, President and Founder Pinnacle Coaching, and author of The Brink; How Great Leadership Is Invented*

"We transform the world by transforming ourselves. And in Fictional Authenticity, Alex guides us through life-affirming practices **to powerfully shift from where we are to where we'd like to be.** Throughout the journey, he gently guides us to **step into our power & own our impact.**"

- **David Ji**, *award winning author of Sacred Powers and the best-selling author of Destressifying*

"Alex is a coach I deeply respect for his commitment to mastering his craft by investing the time and training to facilitate deep transformation in his clients lives. **He is one of the few coaches today who prioritizes serving over selling.**"

- **Peter Scott IV**, *best-selling author of The Fearless Mindset and Founder of Fearless Life Academy*

"Alex Terranova is a brilliant, joyful and **boldly dynamic coach with a keen ability to cut-through the bullshit and create powerful change** in the lives of others. His commitment to authentic transformation is exceptional; his strategies and advice serve as a supportive mirror, your biggest cheerleader and the motivation to elevate to your very best. I would highly recommend this book to anyone looking for **meaningful growth and to cultivate greater success in their personal or professional lives.**"

- **Corene Summers,** *International Meditation Teacher and Founder of The Artisan Pharmacy*

"Alex is truly a one-of-a-kind, no-nonsense, heart-centered, spirit-led kind of guy. And it's a pleasure and privilege to know him as a friend.

In addition to the **treasure trove of timeless wisdom and sage advice that he offers,** what inspires me most about Alex and this phenomenal book, is his **authentically gritty and bold - but loving - voice!** That, more than anything else, separates him from the other extraordinary self-help experts in the field.

Alex genuinely strives to make people's lives better, and he's committed to practicing what he preaches; he walks the talk because he's done - and continues doing - the work. And that makes all the difference in the world.

This is a real book for real people - people like you, me and Alex. With this book, Alex didn't just put his thoughts on paper; he put **his entire heart and soul into these pages.** In doing so, he shares not only his own fascinating personal journey but also **practical tips, tricks, tools, and techniques for carving out your own authentic path to true success and authentic happiness, too.**"

- **Robert Mack,** *author of Happiness from the Inside Out, Positive Psychology Expert & host of Good Morning LaLa Land*

FICTIONAL AUTHENTICITY

Release Your Past,
Start Living Your Real Life

Alex Terranova

Alex Terranova

Paperback: ISBN 978-1-6928068-4-2

Editing by Christina Stathopoulos
Book Cover Design: Jess Fang
Photo: Susan Magnano

www.thedreammason.com

@InspirationalAlex (Instagram) #DreamMason #FictionalAuthenticity

MEDIA + SPEAKING: please contact media@thedreammason.com
ALL INQUIRES: www.thedreammason.com

Published by Accomplishment Media, PO Box 91471 San Diego, CA 92169
www.accomplishmentmedia.com

DEDICATION

◆ ◆ ◆

I could not have written this book without support. I'm being so serious right now. I could not have! That would have been an actual miracle.

There are so many people to thank because without each and every one of you these words and ideas would not have reached the page. Okay, well maybe they would have reached the page, but in a way in which the grammar, punctuation, and syntax was so amiss nobody would ever dare to read it.

I want to thank everyone at Accomplishment Coaching, the world's finest coach training program. Thank you to Christopher for creating and leading a program that literally changes people's lives, and for changing my life. For being a mentor, a friend, a leader, and a stand for all that is possible in my life and in the world. Christopher, thank you for pushing me, always believing in me, inviting me to co-host The Coaching Show podcast with you, and giving The DreamMason Podcast a home. While nobody could ever replace my Father, thank you for providing that fatherly brand of love, humor, and support. This book wouldn't exist if it weren't for what I learned from Accomplishment

Coaching, from you, and through the breakthroughs I created in the process.

Thank you, Kerry, for truly seeing me and being the most wickedly powerful woman I've ever encountered.

Liz, I started writing this book in Queens, NY. It wouldn't exist without who you were for me then. Thanks for being fierce and loving, for believing in me when I didn't at all believe in myself. Thanks for never seeing me as the jerk that I thought I was, for accepting me exactly as I was and never needing me to change or transform.

Thank you, Kacey, my first coach. I wouldn't have become a coach if it weren't for that epic sample session you provided in Brooklyn roughly 5 years ago. Thanks for loving me through one of the most challenging times of my life. Thank you for showing me that I was capable of quitting a job and creating my own business, and for reminding me that I'm a writer and pushing me to create the first draft of this book. Thanks for always getting me, I know at times I didn't make it easy.

Thank you Ian, Jonas, Lee, Seb, and Ray for being great friends who always supported me as I figured my shit out.

Thank you to Elena, Cailin, Emily, Robbi, Jeff, and Cat. You have been my life jackets, keeping me above water when I forgot who I was, when I quit on myself, when highs turned to lows, when I said fuck everyone and everything. I'm grateful for you all.

Nikki & Chris, I love that you loved me even when I was a little jerk. A human couldn't ask for a better and more fun Aunt and Uncle. Thanks for introducing me to the law of attraction and personal growth so long ago. It was a game changer.

Chelsea, thanks for being fearless. For asking the perfect question at the perfect moment.

Daniel, aka best little brother, I love you, thanks for supporting me through my growth, the changes I've made, and always loving me even when we were kids and I bullied you.

Hollie, thanks for always reminding me to not listen to the negative self talk. Thanks for the daily support, the filming videos, the pep talks, the love. Thanks for pushing me to be the extraordinary man that you tell me I am.

Mark, thank you for teaching me and modeling integrity, commitment, and powerful vulnerable masculine love. Thanks for never quitting on me, regardless of the messes I made. Thanks for having the same conversations with me over and over again about self-love, trust, faith, and commitment so I could be the man I needed to be to create this book. You are not only an amazing coach, but a Beast and an Angel for your clients.

Melanie, I think you might be my Guardian Angel. You came into my life when things were bleak, we created a friendship and have supported each other through dark and light, love and heartbreak and everything in between. Thanks for helping with this book but mostly for being a daily reminder of what it means to come from love and possibility.

Brittany, I don't know how you put up with me. I'm the best or the worst and you deal with all of it almost every day. You are more than just a cousin, you are a friend, a confidant, a drinking buddy, a complaining buddy, a yoga buddy, and someone I rely on to tell me what's what no matter how much of a dick I might be. Thanks for bringing the love and joy that is little Teddy, into our lives. Thanks for trusting me and giving always giving me the room to be my authentic self.

Christina, my co-pilot! I am really glad I made a slot for you in my calendar. This book wouldn't be published if it weren't for your commitment to me, my words, and what's possible through transformation for others. It doesn't make sense that we became friends, almost like family at this point. Or that your Mom is my podcast's #1 fan. And it makes even less sense that you said yes to taking this book on as a project with me. You put up with all the non-sense, complaints, "poor me" bullshit I bring and make fun of me for it. You are mighty and fierce, loving and bold. You are a Lioness for the potential of human beings, and you have been that for me. I will never be able to repay you for the time, effort and love you have put into this book, but I will do my best to support you in your life as you have supported me in mine.

Mom & Dad, I love you. I wouldn't be here without you. Dad, thanks for teaching me about hard work, always saying there is no try, just do it. For the hours and hours you've spent supporting me, practicing with me, listening to me, and believing in me. I know you believe I can do and accomplish anything, and it makes me believe in myself a little bit more. Mom, thanks for making sure I wasn't a fucking idiot. For making sure I did those eye exercises, for getting me the tutors and help I needed, for re-writing every single essay I ever wrote. For reading every page of this book and giving an exorbitant number of notes. Great buildings have massive support beams that run through them to keep them standing. You have been that support beam for me and my life. I exist in the capacity to write, to think, to create, because of the support you have provided.

FOREWORD

◆ ◆ ◆

When my son, Alex, asked me to write the Foreword to his first book, I had two feelings simultaneously. I felt honored and terrified.

I was honored, who wouldn't be, that my son wanted me to be part of his endeavor. And, I was terrified that my attempt wouldn't be what he or others expected, or it just wouldn't be good enough, by which I mean "perfect." After all, I was a Mom, teacher, businesswoman, Executive Director of several community-based counseling and training centers, and a Licensed Marriage & Family Therapist. I was not a writer. What did I know about writing a Foreword?

Later that morning, while doing the brunch dishes, an unusual thought surprised me.

Alex's book, in essence, is about loving and trusting oneself. It is about opening possibilities by stepping out of your comfort zone to do something you want to do and are afraid to do. I decided at that moment that the best way to honor my son and his ideas was to show that the changes he made in his life, in his relationships, and espoused in this book, made a recognizable impact on my life, and I believe will have a positive impact on the lives of others.

He inspired me to be courageous enough to step out of my comfort zone to commit to doing something that I really wanted to do and was afraid to do...write this Foreword.

As you will discover when reading Fictional Authenticity, Alex's book is a reflection of the knowledge and experiences he gained that altered his beliefs about himself, his attitudes, his behavior, and his view of society, religion and spirituality. Most importantly, this transformation changed the way he defined, and continues to define, success and joy.

Fictional Authenticity is Alex's gift to those still struggling to discover who they really are, who they want to be and how to create the life of their dreams. Astronaut Buzz Aldrin said, "your mind is like a parachute: if it isn't open, it doesn't work."

Alex truly believes you can have the life you want. He just asks that you open your mind and believe it too.

Sandy Terranova

To my Grandparents, Lee and Sylvia

"With the fear of being punished and the fear of not getting the reward, we start pretending to be what we are not, just to please others, just to be good enough for someone else. We try to please Mom and Dad, we try to please the teachers at school, we try to please the church, and so we start acting. We pretend to be what we are not because we are afraid of being rejected. The fear of being rejected becomes the fear of not being good enough. Eventually we become someone we are not. We become a copy of Mamma's beliefs, Daddy's beliefs, society's beliefs, and religion's beliefs."

- DON MIGUEL RUIZ, THE FOUR AGREEMENTS

PREFACE

◆ ◆ ◆

"This is a book about discovering who you are, who you've always been, embracing, loving and expanding it. You are enough. You are pure love. Everything you need, you already are. Go share your gifts with the world because there is no one else like you."

- ALEX TERRANOVA

E veryone has a voice in their head. Everyone has a voice in their heart.

You are likely more familiar with the voice in your head.

Sometimes it sounds like it hates you.

It is a doubting, criticizing, horrible, sneaky, consoling, worrisome, malevolent, sad, and righteous voice. If anyone else spoke to you in the way this voice did—every day, all the time, over and over again—at the very least you would try to avoid them, shut them out, or even fight them. If a parent spoke to a child that way, it would be abuse. If a boss verbally shits on an employee the way that voice shits on us, eventually there'd be a major lawsuit.

If you do not know that voice, you are lucky. Maybe you

have found great ways to block it out, or maybe it's just become so normal that you don't even question it.

I invite you to question it now.

What is that voice?

Who is that voice?

For some of us, it is loud. For others, it whispers. It judges. It worries. For some of us, it tells us to be louder and speak up. For others, it says stay quiet, do not get noticed. It says whether to agree or disagree. For some of us, it pushes us, and for others, it seems to hold us back.

That voice tells us that we *can't*, or that we *aren't good enough*. It reminds us that we aren't smart enough or pretty enough, that we are too fat or too thin. It looks for who to blame for life not being easier or better. Maybe it blames our parents, the schools, the government, or even God for our problems.

Do you know the voice now?

Right now, mine is talking to me. It is telling me how hard this is going to be. That nobody will publish me anyway and that nobody cares what I have to say. It tells me I am not smart enough, not a good enough writer, too young, or not experienced enough.

For as long as I can remember, it has always told me that I am not enough.

I remember asking my first coach, "Am I good enough to do this?"

I know that many of us ask ourselves that same question. But we rarely ask, why?! And who determines the answer to that anyway?

We are not here to do only the things we are good or great

at. We are here to experience life, and if that means there is something you want or something you want to do, nothing, no one, no fears or doubts, not even the voice in your head should stop you.

So many of us are stopped by the voice in our head. Maybe it is not an everyday thing, but at some point, or another the voice in our head tells us to stop, to quit, that we cannot, that we are not good enough, or we are just not enough. It has us play small, stay in jobs we don't love, date the wrong people, and self-sabotage our health and well-being. It can even keep us blind to what we really want.

This voice is the reason that so many of us have accepted lives that we are not loving. It is the reason we are not achieving our goals and striving for our dreams. Likely it is the reason we distract ourselves with hours of TV, video games and social media. At least when we are distracted that voice is quiet.

That voice is like a cancer and it is fed by our fears, insecurities, and others' opinions. It will stop at nothing to keep us exactly where we are, safe and stagnant, in our comfort zones.

When I realized that voice was not who I was meant to be and was keeping me from realizing my greatness and potential, I knew I had to write this book.

At the end of the day it does not matter if only one books sells (my Mom, thanks Mom) or thousands of books sell. Yes, I would love if this book impacted people's lives and they took powerful insights away from it that impacted their lives in a positive way. And I am truly writing this book for me because the voice says, I shouldn't, I can't, I'm not good enough or smart enough to do it.

But my heart tells me over and over again to write.

We need to chase our dreams without stopping because of the voice in our head!

This book is dedicated to every single person in the world. Every person that ever lived before me and that will live after me that hears the voice in their head that stands between them and the life they want to be living. To every person that's been battling with it. To every person that has been tormented by it. To every person who has let it control or even ruin their lives. To every person who did not or is not pursuing their purpose, goals, dreams or passions, all because of this fucking voice!

And mostly, to everyone who does not feel like they truly and deeply love themselves.

This book is for you. It is for us. It is for the voice. Because when we do things like this, we actually take back power from the voice.

This book is about creating your life differently and falling in love with your life and with yourself.

It is about choosing what you want and taking action to achieve it.

It is about interrupting your thoughts, which become your beliefs, that inspire your actions and therefore create the life you are living.

It is about realizing that joy, fulfillment, inner peace, and success is inherently available to all of us, but it is 100% up to us to create it!

We have forgotten who we are. We have forgotten that we are more than just blood and bones and muscles and organs. We have forgotten that we are great. That we are divine. That we are creators. We have forgotten to dream and believe in the impossible. We have forgotten that life is not given to us so we can sit behind a desk and work only to get that paycheck only to want more and more and more. We are not meant for the lives most of us are living...

We have forgotten that "we are not human beings having a spiritual experience; we are spiritual beings having a human experience." (Pierre Teilhard de Chardin)

This book is a reminder that life isn't about discovering who you are or what you are here for...

You are simply alive to create your life.

You will look within and remember that your ability to create has always been there.

You will see that it exists in our hearts, our minds, and our souls. It is embedded in our dreams and shows up through our creativity. It is built into our passion and our purpose.

Life is ours to believe, create, and sculpt into reality.

This book is about taking responsibility for your life and unleashing The DreamMason® inside of you...

Because Your Dreams Don't Build Themselves!

1 | WAKE UP!

◆ ◆ ◆

"Changing is not just changing the things outside of us. First of all, we need the right view that transcends all notions including being and non-being, creator and creature, mind and spirit. That kind of insight is crucial for transformation and healing."

- THICH NHAT HANH

Bottom line. *This chapter is like an alarm clock for your life. And guess what, it's time to wake up. This chapter is about:*

- *Realizing that most of our lives are completely predictable*
- *Understanding how predictable lives lead to inauthentic lives*
- *Uncovering how Life could be a Choose Your Own Adventure*
- *Acknowledging that we avoid choice because of fear*
- *Getting that for changes to happen, we must be willing*

PUNCHED IN THE NOSE

I sat there unable to speak. Tears rolled down my face, I was choked up and could not get a word out. My family stared at me confused, shocked and yet compassionate and connected to me. I did not have any idea at that moment why I was crying, what I wanted to say or what was actually going on.

And let me be clear, I wasn't just crying, I was balling. I was seriously choked up. This was not something that happens. Shit, I'm a man, a masculine one, and up until that point one who didn't feel much.

I was lucky. I "woke up" right before my 33rd birthday. Some of us never wake up. Some of us wake up so late in our lives we are left with a life of regrets. And it's never too late to wake up.

I wish I could say why I woke up or why at that moment. I believe life provides us with moments, new paths to either utilize or step over. It's consistently doing it and often we are choosing to stay on the path we are on because to change is uncomfortable and often scary.

For some reason in that moment, I chose to step off my path and step onto a vastly different one.

We cannot force waking up on others. It is like in the movie The Matrix, when Neo has the choice to take the red pill. He is not forced, he cannot be made to, but if he does pick it, and he chooses to take a look at life with fresh new eyes, with a new perspective there will be no going back.

For me there was no red pill or a blue pill or any pill for that matter. Unfortunately, Lawrence Fishburne was not there or even narrating it. That would have been pretty cool.

For me, waking up, coming alive again happened one December night in Costa Rica.

I sat at a dimly lit open-air fish restaurant with my family. We had been told it was a good place, but a spiritual awakening was not promised, on the menu or even part of the plan.

And that likely was a good thing, if it had been, I probably would have ordered the burger instead.

From the moment we arrived in Costa Rica, I had started to badger my then girlfriend about moving there.

Wait...

I should step back.

LIFE IS PREDICTABLE

I was not really asking to move there. I did not realize it at the time, but I was asking to run away there. Inside of the promise of a glamorous beach life, I was actually asking her to run away with me from my problems, my fears, my doubts about achieving my goals, my unhappiness and the other pressures of the world.

Our lives are pretty predictable. Most of the time it is going to go the way it has always gone. Until we do something big, bold, different, or crazy to change it. But most of us will never do that. Most of us do not even know where to start. Most of us will just sleepwalk through our lives. Most of us will work the same or similar jobs and complain about it our entire lives. Most of us will work and work and work hoping one day we can get ahead and retire. We will spend our lives complaining or pretending that the way we are living is really what we deeply want and desire.

People are offering each other opportunities all the time and most of us just pass them up for all sorts of reasons, fear that we might be getting sold something, that we will not like it, maybe that we will not be good at it, or possibly that we did not have the best experience in the past with something similar. We so often hide and steer ourselves away from things that would shake up our lives and then complain that our lives are not what we want them to be.

Sometimes, if we kick the can down the road long enough life gets sick of our bullshit and steps in. Unfortunately, when it goes down like that it is not always pretty. It could be car accident, a near death experience, a big job loss, a sickness, or losing a great love. It is like life sticks a crowbar into our life and thrusts a door open for us. Sometimes we get lucky and it kicks the door open but gives us the opportunity to step through it. Other times it grabs us by the belt and collar and throws us through.

But most of the time, we avoid the ride, we don't go through the door. We stay stuck, stagnate and do roughly the same thing for years. We call that completely predictable routine a life.

Some of us are fine with it, others do not even know it is happening and then there are those of us too consumed by fear and circumstances to actually do anything about it.

Sometimes life just has to shake up our snow globe. For those of us that are lucky, life gives us a glimpse, a peak, or an awareness. We get the opportunity to wake up! Life opens the door and points through it and even has get us very clear on how it has not and is not going to work the ways of the past. Even with that it is still up to us to step through it and keep going.

The magic of Costa Rica was life's crowbar, and the awareness of the life I was living was enough to know I could not go back to New York living the same way.

While life woke me up, I still had to put my feet on the floor and get out of the bed.

I was given the opportunity for my life to be different. I was given the opportunity to change, to transform. Maybe I was asking for it in ways I did not even see. But it's clear I was given a chance to shake my own snow globe and recreate my life. I am so grateful I did not have to be faced with death or a tragedy to see how ugly or scary the bottom could be.

I believe we are all consistently given opportunities like this. Often, they are subtle offerings from others, opportunities and choices we turn down. An evening out instead of staying in could lead to meeting that special someone. Choosing to go on that hike or to that class instead of watching TV, could lead to weight loss, a new skill or passion and who knows what shows up from there.

We have opportunities every day to choose to change our direction, create a new path, and while they seem scary, difficult, and involve taking a risk, they do exist.

And I want to be super clear, I'm not writing this with the message that if you are homeless, starving, don't have clean water or other basic needs that changing your life is easy or just a mindset shift. I'm writing this book and generating these conversations for people that have jobs, have shelter, food, have their basic needs met...and honestly, most of the people who have picked this book up, purchased it, have their basic needs met.

Sitting at that restaurant in Costa Rica, God, the Universe, Spirit or whatever you want to call it decided it was time to open the door.

Now it would be my choice to step through or not.

As I sat there balling...I felt a profound opportunity had arisen. Something had shifted. I could see the faces of my cousins, my parents, my Aunt and Uncle, and my girlfriend. They all looked shocked, surprised, vulnerable, sad and yet compassionate. I do not believe that they had ever seen me open up and cry like that besides at my grandparents' funerals.

In general, I did not cry. I did not breakdown. I was always very strong, and I could power through most things. I was a tank, I moved through situations and got to the other side without letting my heart be exposed.

The Universe laughs at people like me. It laughs as we miss massive experiences to feel this life. It laughs as think we have it figured out.

We are not human doings!

We are human beings!

And Being is all about feelings, connection and relationship to ourselves and others.

What triggered my crying came from my cousin asking everyone at the table what they were grateful for.

This was not odd for my family. My Mom would often do this at holiday meals and still does up until this day. When someone would ask, usually my brother or I would shoot back jokes about dicks, sex, pooping because of coffee, or something else that was silly, immature and childish.

Well not this time...

This time the Universe landed an opened handed smack to my face.

I do not even know what I said. I think I said I was grateful for them, our health, our financial security and for my girlfriend for putting up with all my bullshit and giving me the opportunity to grow up. And it does not matter what I said, what matters is how I was moved. The question itself shifted something inside of me, which I was not willing to ignore.

In hindsight I believe I know what happened. For the first time in my life, I realized how lucky I was. I was living in Brooklyn, New York at the time, working a really good job that I did not like, making good money that I did not think was enough, and complaining regularly about how life "should" be or how people "should" be or what I "should" have.

In that moment I got Scrooged. I didn't get a cool visit from 3 angels, but I could see all the sides of my life all the same time. In that moment I became aware that the way I was living was bullshit. It was empty, hollow, stagnant and leading nowhere except to more of the same feelings of dissatisfaction. I saw that I had everything to be grateful for and fuck me for not appreciating any of it.

In that moment I knew I was living life inauthentically, without joy and not living the life I wanted to be living.

CHOOSE YOUR OWN ADVENTURE

When I was a kid, I loved reading Choose Your Own Adventure novels. I remember the hero reaching crossroads and the simple prompt of "turn to this page." Turn to page 58 if you want to chase the bad guy into the diamond mine. Turn to page 72 if you want to rescue the girl. It was always up to you to choose.

I think those books are life.

Life is a fucking Choose Your Own Adventure novel!

Think about it, you wake up tomorrow and decide to just say fuck it and not go to work and instead go to the airport with one bag and buy a one-way ticket to Australia!

Ok that's extreme. Maybe you wake up tomorrow and go workout, you meditate, you make up with a friend or family member you've been fighting with. Maybe you eat healthy, start writing that book you've been talking about or start looking for a job you might love.

Any of those things...

And boom! A huge change in the direction of your life.

From here who knows what happens next. Everything suddenly becomes unpredictable.

That's choosing your own adventure. Adventure is not knowing what will happen next. Adventure is a willingness to let go, surrender and live. Adventure is choosing to go in an unknown direction where the future is going to revel itself to you as a complete surprise.

I wouldn't be stretching it to say that barely any of us live like that. Most of us don't even think about it and wouldn't even consider it. We would call it crazy. Yeah, we all know someone who lives the "Choose Your Own Adventure life" and maybe we tell them they are lucky or amazing or maybe we call them irresponsible or try to point out that their lives are different, and they don't have the responsibilities we have. We always have to give reason or justify why we can't or why others can.

Why aren't we all living our dream from a Choose Your Own Adventure life?

Because we're scared. Because we are logical, and we think with our heads and not our hearts. We're afraid we'll lose our job. Afraid what people might think about us. We might be thinking we can't, that's not responsible and we'll mess up all our career growth. Or maybe it's I can't afford it.

Life has the potential to be a Choose Your Own Adventure Novel.

But not for most of us. Most of us are stuck with fine when we could have great. Most of us would rather keep living as Clarke Kent than ever accept that deep down we are Superman!

Because of fear!

Fucking *fear*!

So how does fear play into my life and waking up? Well I didn't know it at the time. At the time I was telling myself I couldn't open my own business as I didn't have the money. I was saying I couldn't travel all over the world for fun as I didn't have the money. I could come up with all the reasons or circumstances to stand in the way of the life I wanted to live.

It was easier not to try. Easier to pretend life was fine and I didn't need or want the things my soul was yearning for.

Sound familiar?

To bring it back to this moment the tears in Costa Rica, I realized I was at a crossroads of my own Choose Your Own Adventure.

If I chose to go back to New York and kept living the same life everything was pretty predictable. While it would have been fine, it would not have been great. It likely would have led to a moderately successful life that was mostly unfulfilling, without a sense of genuine well-being and joy.

However, if I used this experience to turn to hypothetical page 85 and made a big change, I had no idea what might happen. But if I was willing to try something different to make new choices, do more self-reflection, and take some risks, I would see joy, happiness, satisfaction and fulfillment as a reality.

I didn't know how or what would make those things part of my new story, but I knew if I kept reading the same chapter over and over again nothing was going to change. I had to be willing to let go and jump into unfamiliar territory.

The Universe shook open my life and asked me to make a choice. It was my little prompt at the bottom of the page. Stay here and you know how it's going to go or turn to page 85 but you don't know what will happen, but you know it means stepping into new possibility.

I chose to turn to page 85. I chose to shake my snow globe. I chose to run through that fucking door.

This is the journey of how and why I did it, and how you can choose freedom, joy, self-love, relationships, and connection. This is your first step in starting to live your dreams and letting love and possibility flow through you.

YOUR TURN:

1) Are you willing to accept that you have been living a predictable life, a life that is inside your comfort zone, a life where you aren't fully following your heart?

Hell Yes or *No* (Circle one)

If *No*, close this book immediately and give it to a friend. If *Hell Yes*, proceed to #2.

2) Take out a piece of paper and write down your answers to these prompts. Don't let it take you more than one page, you can go back and add to this later.

   a) What does the voice in your head tell you about who you are?

   b) What beliefs are you clinging to, and how do those beliefs keep you safe?

   c) What woke you up?

   d) What did you learn or realize about your life and yourself?

3) Take out another piece of paper. Describe the last big dream you had. Add as much detail as you need to really feel connected to it again.

4) If you don't believe you are "awake" yet, write down all the reasons why it's benefiting you to stay stuck, distracted, or unaware of your greatness and potential. And consider you are awake, buying this book is evidence of that as you clearly want things to go differently.

2 | HOW LIFE GOT THIS WAY

◆ ◆ ◆

"In evolutionary history, threats usually had more impact on survival opportunities. Sticks are more salient than carrots: So the amygdala is primed to label experiences negatively. The amygdala-hippocampus systems flags negative experiences primarily in memory. So the brain becomes like velcro for negative experience but teflon for positive ones. Consequently, the avoid system routinely hijacks the approach and attach systems and bad is just stronger than good."

- DR. RICK HANSON

Bottom line. *Your life didn't just happen. You created it. Well, with the help of the world around you. This chapter is all about:*
- *Understanding how the hell things got this way*
- *Recognizing when in time the world was no longer safe for us*
- *Seeing how we create stories about our safety to protect ourselves from what we fear*

Alex Terranova

- *Defining our Fear Stories*
- *Piecing together how Fear Stories create Fictional Authenticity*

HERE'S WHAT HAPPENED,
WITH SCIENCE!

How did life get this way?

Why would this crazy world, this crazy life we live set us up like this?

Well, let's take a look at the human being through a developmental lens.

We are born. When we are young, we don't have access to much information. Our brains are not developed and while they support survival functions like breathing, digestion, etc. our logical and cognitive functions are far from being developed.

There comes a point around two or three years old where we start to develop the ability to form and hold long-term memories. Our implicit and explicit memories. And studies have suggested that babies that aren't held, loved or connected to the heart beats of their mothers after birth have emotional and developmental issues as they grow up. They might not have an explicit memory of what happened when they were babies, but there is a knowing, known as implicit memory, that goes beyond traditional memory.

I want to remind you to put this book into the context of where it's being written and who is reading it. If you were living in extreme poverty or danger or without food or clean water, this book is not intended for you. As Indian Guru and Mystic Sadhguru says, "I am speaking to a bloated population in their bellies and minds." What that means is I'm talking to those of you that own the latest iPhones, Androids, or belong to gyms where you pay lots of money to lift things and run in place. Those of us who have privileged lives.

28

Similarly, I'm not speaking to those of us that had severe trauma as children, especially those who had trauma prior to explicit memory. If you went through traumatic experiences, there was likely an impact far beyond the scope of this book. While aspects might apply to you, what you have experienced is beyond my sphere of knowledge or expertise.

While we have explicit memory before 3 years old most of us start to create the stories about how life is and how we are between the ages of two and six years old. Typically, between those ages the world stops feelings safe, cozy, and reliable.

So, what happened?

When we were young, ideally speaking we were safe and taken care of. Someone held us, rocked us, protected us, fed us, cleaned us, sang to us, read to us, walked around with us, and held us close to their beating heart.

Was all of this the experience for all of us? No, of course not. However, this was the ideal and most of us experienced enough of this to develop as we would prefer.

At some point in the journey we began to separate ourselves a little. Not much at first. At some point we started walking, talking, moving around, feeding ourselves, and saying "No" and then yes.

In childhood development, we would say, we no longer were in a symbiotic relationship and we began to develop a self, separate from our mother. Through this new lens the world is different.

As an independent self and through our experiences we started crafting original thoughts and ideas about life, others, situations, and who we are. Those ideas and stories molded and created the lens we grow up seeing the world through.

Just this morning my Aunt was telling me a story about her dog on the beach. Skipper was having the time of his life being off his leash, when he spotted a little boy and sprinted off to him. My Aunt wasn't worried about Skipper, she knew he probably just wanted to play or lick the boy's face. But she also knew this boy was young and could easily be scared, and likely the chance of him being frightened would also scare his mother who was just a few feet away.

That's exactly what happened.

Skipper licked the little boy's face. The little boy freaked out and started to cry. The mother panicked, and even while realizing her son was fine was left with "but what if..." anxiety. My Aunt apologized, because while she knew it was never Skipper's intent to scare the boy, that was the result. She even offered to hold Skipper and let the little boy pet him to see that Skipper was safe, because my Aunt recognized that this little boy could create a story around this and fear dogs for the rest of his life.

I love this story, because this is life, and this is what happens to us when we are young. Random, totally normal things that our brains can't process or understand, become the stories and meanings our minds create about things to make them make sense. Maybe this little boy creates a story about how dogs aren't safe, or animals are unpredictable. Maybe he even makes it mean that his mother can't protect him, and he has to be on the defensive all the time. Or maybe he creates a story that dangerous things can appear out of nowhere at any time and it's always safer to be guarded and on your toes.

There are a million stories that a mind can create from this, none of which are wholly true, but all have a lasting impact.

Now, armed with this story, this little boy will walk out into the world and his brain, his subconscious mind, will look for evidence that supports the belief that he made up. It will look at all situations through this lens and accept information that supports his beliefs and disregard information that doesn't fit this belief.

Can you see how wild, crazy and yet impactful this is on who we are? The things that happen to us when we are little, and as we mature, leave an unintentional lasting impact on who we become.

I'm using an example that is super innocent and only one incident in what is a life filled with many "incidents" that build on each other. They reinforce the meaning of the story we created. So, imagine if we grew up in a house where our parents used violence to punish us, or a house where our parents fought continuously. What stories would we make up about life from those experiences. What stories would we make up about big brothers that bully us, or big sisters that control us, or kids that don't accept us, or when we get don't get picked for a team, or when we get criticized...

I think you get it. Regular, dramatic and traumatic things happen to us when we are young; it's life and whether it's acceptable or not, it leaves our young minds creating stories, which creates the lens or perspective in which we will see the world.

Unfortunately, the basis or core of these past stories is almost always based in fear...

FEAR AND THE EGO

We are all afraid all the time.

Everything is based on two basic emotions, fear and love.

We are afraid of not being liked or being judged. We are afraid of falling, sky-diving, skateboarding, sharks, planes, heights, snakes and insects. We are afraid of not being good enough or being ugly or too skinny or too fat. We are afraid our clothes won't fit us right or we'll fail the test, or we won't get the job. We are afraid we are bad parents or bad partners. We are afraid of what will happen if "that" politician gets elected.

We are afraid we'll cheat or get cheated on. Maybe we are afraid we might get bored of the person we love. Or afraid we'll actually love this person forever. Sometimes we are even afraid that if we accomplished our goals, who would we be then? Will our family and friends still accept us? We are afraid to choose. We are afraid of missed opportunities, taking advantage of opportunities or that we'll never get the opportunity. We are even afraid to say, *Yes* or to say *No*.

When you are thinking about quitting your job and you don't move forward with it, you might come up with all these great reasons for not quitting. In actuality at the root you are scared, worried, or maybe doubting your ability to make money on your own or get another job. Whatever it is, it's stemming from fear.

Take something you want to be doing. Right now, think about something you want to be doing and that you are not doing. Try this! Think about the reason that you have used, or the circumstances which are stopping you. Be honest about them, and then look further, what is actually in the way. If you are stuck, notice you are simply buying into the stories, the feelings or the circumstances as real. Yes, they feel real, but when you get down to the nitty gritty, you are just stopped by fear.

And it's cool. It's normal. If there only is fear and love, we fall to one side or the other. But the thing is fear isn't real. It doesn't produce anything, it just stops things.

Let's look more at this and at love.

We are love, and love is everywhere and somehow still we have been groomed, conditioned and sucked into the cyclone of fear. I know this because look how we start. As babies all of us are perfect, pure, love, and joy. We only start to be something else due to the circumstances, traumas, and challenges we face.

Spiritually, it is because fear keeps us separate from the divine, from the universe, from each other, from God. It doesn't matter what you believe, fear separates us from everything. It has us feel alone, not like others, on the defense pushing others away. Fear will never bring us closer together.

So, from a spiritual perspective, if we didn't have fear, we would realize our divinity and our connection to each other as one, and we would simply be. Our Ego uses fear to keep us separate, to keep us from knowing and understanding who we truly are, which is love.

Some of you are saying, I'm not afraid. I'm not separate. But consciously or not we are afraid. We are afraid of things like crime and terrorism. We are afraid of our kids being shot in schools. Or maybe we are afraid the government is going to take our guns.

The point is, we are afraid of good things and bad things. We are afraid of scary things and not so scary things. We are afraid of things outside of us and things inside of us. We are afraid of things that are silly and things that are violent. We are afraid of love and afraid of not getting love.

But we are afraid, and that is the fear.

What we are most afraid of is just being ourselves. Being authentic. Telling the person, we love how we feel. Dancing and totally letting loose. Singing or sharing our art or creative ventures with the world. Chasing the big, huge audacious dream that our heart yearns for. We are afraid that if we actually took off our masks we wouldn't be liked or loved or accepted.

We are so afraid that we've crafted our whole personalities around protecting ourselves from all that we fear. We've created Fictionally Authentic lives as a defense against these fears. But the funny thing is in creating these stories to protect ourselves we have actually actualized these fears and made them real. You don't have to protect yourself against something that isn't real. You only have to protect yourself against an actual threat.

Our fears are not an actual threat, we feel like they are. We experience them as real, but they are made up in our minds. The more we focus on them, the more we separate ourselves from our true self, others, and the universe. And the more these fears become real.

Humans are pretty silly creatures. We make up a story that's based in fear, then we create a whole life around protecting it and proving it to be true.

We all do it. Every one of us. Because nobody escaped childhood unscathed.

Spiritually, we are all one, we are all divine and connected to each other, the world, the universe.

What did the events of our childhood do? They separated us. Before the stories, as a child you played with, loved, connected to, said hi, and were so open to create instant relationships with others. Then these events began, and we created stories that divided us. The story based in fear is designed to keep us safe, forget where we come from, forget that we are all in this together, and that we are pure love, and everything is pure love.

And now the Ego has a job. The Ego has something to do. It has the job of keeping us "safe" and separate, even separate from ourselves. If we cannot connect to ourselves, how can we deeply connect with others and share ourselves with others? If we are separate and unexposed even to our imperfect selves, we are safe.

MEANING MAKING MACHINES

The brilliant author, spiritual leader and speaker Michael Bernard Beckwith maintains,

"In an evolutionary context, one purpose of the ego was to protect our individual identity, to recognize the difference between ourselves and a poisonous plant, aggressive animals, other tribes that could be dangerous to our tribe-things of that nature. Today's evolutionary progress requires that we transcend the ego and realize our Oneness with all beings, with all life. When we do so, we will cease being frightened by our individual differences... The root of ego is that we exist as a self separate from the Whole. Relating to ourselves in this way, 'survival of the fittest' approach seems unnecessary. All this does is give birth to fear, anxiety, mistrust, and greed based on a false sense that there is not enough good to go around so we must hoard and protect how little or how much is in our possession."

We aren't breaking up with our ego anytime soon. We can become more aware of it, more mindful, do the work to keep it in check, but it actually exists to protect us.

Think about this through the context of one of the first

words we learn. *No.* How do we learn it? Because as we learned to crawl and move around and start doing things, our parents started telling us no constantly. They did it to keep us safe, to protect us, to teach us rules and keep us inside of boundaries. They mostly did it out of love. And, *No* is built on the back of fear.

It's interesting that one of the first lessons we learn in life is a limiting behavior lesson.

> *"If parents want to give their children a gift; the best gift they can do is to teach their children to love challenges, be intrigued by mistakes, enjoy effort, and keep on learning. That way, their children don't have to be slaves to praise. They will have a lifelong way to build and repair their own confidence."*

> \- CAROL S. DWECK

This is done with the intent to protect and socialize our children. However, the consequence of it is creating a world of people who are socialized in fear, trapped in the past, worried about the present, and anxious about the future.

If we know we are doing this, why do we keep doing it?

We don't know better. We aren't mindful about what we do or say. We often lie or withhold information from children because we've decided they don't need to know? Why? Because we don't want them to worry? Due to our own fear, we feel the need to protect children by setting limiting rules or behaviors.

For example:

"Children should be seen and not heard"

"No, don't touch this or play with that"

"You have to eat all your dinner before you have dessert."

"That's just how men are!"

"That's just how women are!"

"Money doesn't grow on trees!"

I point to all of this because at some point during our childhood, these messages started to impact our psyche. Our belief systems were created around what we feared or worried about. Our self-consciousness began to take shape.

We were teased at school or got lost in the super market, we were hit or punished, or watched our parents fight, and our developing brains were unable to make sense of all of it. We could not comprehend the world around us, and so we started inventing a meaning for everything. We trained ourselves to become meaning making machines.

For example, when we are kids and we hear our parents arguing we don't understand that it might not have anything to do with us. Because we cannot imagine or even conceptualize a world outside of us, it must have to do with us and so we might interpret it as though we did something wrong. We might make this mean we have been bad. We might make it mean the world isn't safe. We might make it mean that our parents are scary or that anger is bad.

When we are told to be quiet, to not be so loud, we might interpret that to mean we should be small, hidden and we learn to not own our voice. When we are lied to or betrayed by someone that we love or we depend on we learn to not trust others, to protect our hearts. Or that our feelings aren't valid and so we don't own our own value.

When we grow up in a house where one of our parents is overly emotional, we might make that mean that emotions are bad. When we grow up watching our parents worry or demonstrate their anxieties or perfection-like qualities, we learn those behaviors and create lives in that fashion or the opposite.

This all creates the fear that lies at the root of what I'm calling our Fictional Authentic Lives.

So now let's look at my fear stories and see if you can get present to your fear story.

FEAR STORIES

My Fear Stories - #1

I want to share with you more of my stories, because I believe it helps illustrate how the fear authors the story of our lives, our Fictional Authenticity. My hope is that as you read about me, you are able to start distinguishing things about your life and how you created and wrote your story. There is no better way to change your story than by first acknowledging that you authored it. From there you can take responsibility and start working on your re-write.

I have three core fear stories that I have identified. There are likely many more as we are complex beings and lots of experiences impacted us early on. But here is what I have come up with so far:

My first story starts with learning that I was broken. Remember, this isn't true, it's the meaning I made as a child from a situation I couldn't understand or comprehend.

When I was about five or six, the eye doctor diagnosed me with having an eye muscle issue. The muscles that helped my eyes move inward and outward didn't work correctly. They were not strong enough, which was impacting my ability to learn how to read.

The good news was that this condition was "fixable." The doctor gave my mom these little prisms and instructed her on how to do daily eye exercises with me to strengthen the muscles. My mom, being the loving, caring, committed mother she was, did these exercises with me every day. In my recollection, we never missed a single day.

That being said, right from that early age, I felt something was wrong with me. Why did I have to do these exercises? Other kids didn't have to.

I was broken.

Now as an adult, if I had been told that my right thigh muscle was weaker than my left, which impacted my walking, I wouldn't relate to myself as broken. I would think, oh my right thigh is weaker than my left. There would be no meaning beyond that, just the fact. Anything else would be considered made up. While it might serve me to strengthen it, my thigh isn't broken, and I am not broken because of it.

As children, we are developing our meaning making machine, so we apply meaning to everything. As children, it's all we have. As adults we can put things that happen into our meaning making machine, but we can also realize that because we got dumped or cheated on that doesn't actually mean we suck at relationships, that's a meaning, an interpretation of an event that is added onto the fact that we got broken up with or cheated on. The meaning isn't true, it's made up.

So, while I was already feeling broken, the work we did was in the hopes of fixing my eyes.

And guess what, we did it! When we went back to the doctor he was blown away. He told my Mom and me that he had never seen 100% recovery and we had 100% recovered.

My Mom fixed me. (That's my story also.)

What I learned and believed was true, was not only had I been broken, but I could be fixed. Some people might read this and think, what's wrong with that? What's wrong with wanting to fix things and take things that aren't working as they should and improve them?

Nothing is wrong with that.

However, as people we aren't broken. That's the misnomer. Consider, we aren't supposed to be any certain way. We come in all shapes, sizes, colors, with different personalities, different mental and physical abilities...everything about us is different and unique.

To say there is a way that a person "should" or "should not" be is simply a judgment or assessment. We might say that it's healthy for a person to be 180lbs if they are 5'11, but that is just a judgment or opinion, it isn't truly a fact. A group of humans somewhere set that standard and we accepted it, but that doesn't make it a fact. There was a time where we accepted that African Americans were 3/5th of a person. That was considered true, but it wasn't a fact. While this is an extreme example, it's no different. Less extreme, that tall people are better, or that women that look like Victoria Secret models are sexier.

We often take opinions, judgments and assessments and label them as facts. When it comes to people, this can play into our Ego's way of keeping us separated and different. It also keeps us separate from ourselves, because if we think we are stupid, broken, different, not good enough, or not worthy, we have trouble loving ourselves.

The idea that someone could be broken is just untrue. And that doesn't mean we can't also grow and improve. They are not mutually exclusive. You can grow and improve without anything being broken or wrong.

I can love my body and still desire it to look, feel or move better. I can run a 5-minute mile and still challenge myself to run a 4-minute mile. My eye muscles can struggle, and I can exercise them to improve their function.

But it becomes a slippery slope for our meaning making machines when we start identifying things as broken and want to fix them.

This is the story that got created in my mind. I believed I was broken, and then I went out into the world with that mind and looked for evidence to prove this story true and ways to fix it when I found it.

It wasn't long before I was diagnosed with some learning disabilities that impacted my ability to read, comprehend and learn. I had a higher than average IQ, but I struggled with comprehension because my brain functioned differently from the average child's.

As an adult, I could receive that information as simply a measurement. Based on an accepted standard, here is where I measured.

But what did I do with information as a kid? I added it to my evidence for why I am broken, why I am not good enough or smart enough.

Yay! More evidence.

As I grew up, feeling broken and not good enough merged with two other powerful stories and started to create the Fictional Authentic life that I would eventually be living.

My Fear Stories - #2

My second fear story involves the first time I made my mark on the world.

When I was about five or six years old, I was getting comfortable writing my name. When you learn to write your name it's a pretty big deal. You get a lot of love for a feat such as that.

Being a showman and wanting to shine, I took a sharpie and wrote my name all over the walls of the house and the garage. I guess I was really proud of myself. I seriously wrote my name everywhere, especially on the outside of the house.

My Dad, a wonderful man, a loving devoted and committed father and husband and the hardest worker I have ever known was the one who discovered my artistic endeavor.

Let's just say he kicked the shit out of me. And honestly, I don't blame him. He's a traditionally masculine man who was raised in a different time in an Italian family where that sort of thing was accepted as normal.

I got it good. And good as in bad.

As I lay crying on the floor of my room, with an ice pack on my back, I stared at a Sports Illustrated Magazine featuring Michael Jordan on the cover. I clearly remember thinking,

One day, I'll show him (my Dad). One day I'll be so great, I'll be this great and then...

I don't remember what came after "and then." But what I see is, I did something I was really proud of and I shared it with the world. As a kid I didn't know this wasn't a good idea or was a problem, I was just following my heart.

And I got hurt for it. Really hurt. By my Dad, someone I really loved.

From this story I learned, be careful about how you leave your mark, it might not be as well received as you think it will be. Those that say they love can hurt you the most.

And somehow, probably because I didn't' understand why I was being punished, this fed my not good enough story because clearly I was formulating the beliefs that if I was great it would in some weird way show my Dad that I was good enough.

These lessons would continue to show up in my life. Everything became about results and proving myself. To silence that voice, I had to be the best and when I wasn't the best, I quit to avoid having the deal with it. I would move from one thing to another attempting to be the best in order to make myself feel like I was enough.

The thing is you can't fill "I am not enough" up with accomplishments, money, success or anything outside of yourself. That's an inside feeling and the only way to fill up that hole is to start falling in love with yourself and to understand that you always have been enough.

I learned that lesson much later. We'll come back to that.

My Fear Stories - #3

Now this third story is the most subtle. And honestly, it's the one I have most recently identified.

I have wonderful parents, they show my brother and me so much love, attention, care and acceptance. They are truly there for us no matter what, love us unconditionally and have sacrificed so much for us. I know how lucky I am when it comes to calling them Mom and Dad.

My Mom is a perfectionist. She is always trying to get it right. And she's smart, focused, committed and resilient so more often than not she does get it right. But the thing is getting it right and being a perfectionist is about control. It's about needing to control the uncontrollable to be safe.

My Mom worries a lot about the future. She worries about

all the things that could possibly go wrong in almost any situation. Having a plan and having it all "figured out" helps her feel in control and helps her avoid potential pitfalls. She also thinks about the past and how things could have gone differently, where she could have done better as a way to make the present more tolerable.

Growing up, I was present to all the controlling and managing that my Mom was always trying to do. I was present to the worry, that there was always a belief that something would likely go wrong. And I was present to the negative bias that looks at all things from what was wrong versus what was right.

As a kid this didn't look fun. It looked hard and stressful, and it didn't make sense.

My Dad was a really hard worker, and he had the idea that life was all about hard work. The harder you worked the more successful you got. Except even though he worked so hard, he never seemed to become rich or a millionaire or something that made that statement completely true.

He also never seemed to be enjoying life. Life always occurred like this thing to grit and bear and work your way through. He had a temper. When he couldn't work things out to his liking, that temper flared. It was scary.

Again, not fun. I wasn't into any of this. His life seemed to be more about suffering than enjoyment. The results he was producing didn't seem to equate to the effort that he was putting out. And I felt afraid of him and his anger.

Basically, between the two of them life or living looked very uncomfortable.

And if you don't want to be uncomfortable, you want to be...

Ding, ding, ding! Comfortable!

That seemed like a way better strategy.

My meaning making machine brain said, being comfortable is a smart, safe and super wise decision. From that moment moving forward I became the Cali-Kid—cool, calm, collected, charismatic. Nothing ever mattered too much, so there was nothing to get too angry or too sad or even too happy about.

But I also always looked good and became super aware of how I looked to others. I kept watch on everything to make sure it all stayed super chill. It was a very good strategy. Just not authentic.

MY FICTIONALLY AUTHENTIC LIFE

Now let's put all three stories together and see what I created.

There was this iconic 80's and 90's TV Show called Saved By The Bell. The lead character was Zack Morris, played by Mark Paul-Gossler. Zack was the stereotype of the smooth, cool, calm, collected guy who had it all figured out. He was popular. He got the girls. And he manipulated everyone to get what he wanted, all the while walking around with that 'my shit don't stink' swagger.

Somewhere in my first 10 years of life, Zack became the default mascot for my identity. I wasn't sitting around thinking I wanted to be like Zack, but I was noticing and watching how this character behaved and was pretty focused on crafting that life for myself.

If you think about it, it covers all my I'm not good enough story bases. I didn't have to be the smartest, which I didn't think I was. I could learn to be charismatic and manipulative and get what I wanted and slip through the cracks where I would have struggled.

I didn't have to be the best at anything because if you're "cool" you can't care too much. This gave me easy outs all over. I didn't need to struggle with my learning disabilities. I didn't need to be angry or sad, disappointed or anxious. It gave me space to be the best, but if I wasn't, I could casually get out of anything.

I'm going to dig into how this evolves and expands over time. My intention is for you to see it so clearly with me that you can start looking for your stories and how you wrote your Fictionally Authentic Life.

As a kid this worked really well in sports. I didn't get rattled. When other kids were crying and couldn't deal with the stress, I loved it. And sometimes I would up the ante and raise the stakes. For example, in baseball I'd walk the bases loaded just to strike the next three batters out.

I don't think I did it consciously, but when the stakes were raised, I got attention. And when I did well in those moments, I was praised. I loved praise. For moments I got to do the impossible. I got to be the hero, unfortunately I didn't realize I was also the villain, setting the hero up.

A few things were happening here. One, I was learning that to feel good about myself, I need to look outside of myself. Internally I felt I wasn't good enough, so I was learning to seek external validation. It's a great sounding strategy... however it doesn't last. But I didn't know that yet.

Another thing I was doing was creating a state where I could raise or lower the bar to get what I needed from others, and sometimes I had the power to control their feelings and get my needs met. Another trap, because if you can't clearly get your own needs met you will ultimately be chasing others for it. I didn't know that yet either.

Remember how I shared that my Dad's temper was scary? Well that works its way in also. See Zack wasn't tough. He was cool and could get out of things, but he wasn't strong. So, like a kid building Legos, I started constructing a more thought out, more powerful personality.

As a kid I didn't want to be scared of my Dad or anyone else, so I had to start crafting new stories. This started a new template in my mind. As a kid this looked like embracing the "bad" --the tattoos, piercings, lifting weights, shaving my head, anything overtly rebellious and masculine.

By the time I was in Junior High, I had the game figured out. I liked girls and they liked me. I was in with the "good" kids the "bad" kids, and the "jocks" so I was safe and comfortable in any environment. I felt like a chameleon at times, being able to fit in anywhere.

But remember what we distinguished about fear. The more we try to protect ourselves from what we fear, the more we make it real. And fear exists to keep us separate from each other. To disconnect us from the truth that we are love.

I had created the perfect protected life to keep myself away from being not good enough, from being told I wasn't great, and from being too worried or working too hard. So inevitably my strategy would run out.

It started in high school.

No 9th grader is the shit. Unless you are a ridiculous athletic prospect at 14, nobody cares about a 9th grader. They aren't the best at sports, they aren't the best with girls, they aren't the smartest, strongest, biggest, or most popular. This was a shock.

It's important to remember this story was all in my head.

You have a story in your head. You had one growing up also.

In my head, I was immediately unnoticed. My stock fell like it was the Great Depression. My confidence and self-worth were put on a strict diet of watery broth, stale bread, and a sprinkling of I'm not good enough.

In 9th grade in sports I suddenly couldn't keep up, everyone else improved while I had been coasting along for far too long. I needed to put in more effort in class or my grades would put me in a spot where my parents would be all over me. But most importantly, I couldn't figure out girls.

See fear has the fucking grand plan, to keep you safe, to keep you repeating the stories you believe are true about life, others and yourself. If fear can create a predictable life then it can feel safe, while also using more fear to keep it that way. I wasn't being totally controlled by fear, but it was driving my life.

I thought I was pulling back and building up the forces. I say this all with a wink and a nod as my conscious brain wasn't planning this but my hyper over active self-awareness muscles were convinced, they were figuring it all out. I was watching everyone. I was hyper aware.

I started becoming friends with girls. I was hearing it right from the source what was good or bad about guys. And while this was great for me on the surface, my fear was taking all the notes and it was unknowingly using it against me. I was crafting a magnificent story that girls liked cool guys, who weren't dumb, but weren't nerdy. They liked athletes, guys who were funny and could make them laugh. They liked nice cars, they liked someone who could make them feel safe.

My brain became a sponge of the male and female dynamic and while I thought it was empowering, it was all driven by fear.

And fear was loving it all. Because deep inside it was validating its claim that I wasn't good enough, good looking enough, muscular enough, strong or fast enough. I wasn't a good enough dancer or smart enough. I wasn't funny enough or rich enough.

If it's not obvious, my fear began to up-level and evolve. What I was most afraid of was not being good enough, but what I wanted most was to be loved and accepted by a girl. I had it that all of my worth was tied up there. I was totally a love-sick puppy dog at heart.

But the fear wasn't going to stand for that. The fear saw love as a boobie trap for suffering. If I let myself get that close to a girl, then I could be crushed. The flood gates of I'm not good enough would be wide open.

So, the fear was using all these stories and opinions to strengthen its judgment muscles. While I had friends, I wasn't creating deep authentic connections. I wasn't comfortable in my own skin, so how could I possibly connect with another?

My fear used my mind to set me up to fail at this game. I had ventured off into the unknown, basically alone and that wasn't the best idea. What did my fear do with this? It locked me up even tighter. It wouldn't let me have fun because of the fear I wouldn't look cool. It wouldn't dare allow me to dance or be silly. It always had me perform so as to appear exactly as the fear would allow.

There is nothing inherently wrong with any of this, except that I wasn't being true to myself and living a life that was truly authentic. I was creating my Fictionally Authentic life. And since I was so young when this started, I couldn't even see the line between fiction and non-fiction.

I don't believe we all need to have three parts, or two parts or ten parts, but the deeper you look, the more you will learn about how you came to be who you think you are, but not who you truly are.

Even as I write this, I am starting to see there are likely even more layers. Don't get caught up in having it all figured out, there is no "there, there". Just be in the process and do the work to discover who you really are.

We all have fear stories that taught us what we need to compensate for in order to feel safe. Acting out in response to these stories gets us something crucial. I get attention. I get to be the good looking, fun, cool guy who has it together. I get noticed by women.

Even if only for moments, our stories teach us a particular way to get our needs met. But remember, they are ruses. When I live in response to my stories, I am not being authentically me. I am getting my needs met as a way to "fix" what I think is wrong with me. Since nothing is actually wrong, playing out this made up story keeps me from getting what I actually need.

As we move further and further through this book, we will continue to break down your stories and limiting beliefs, behaviors and patterns and empower you to create an authentic you, one that is empowered to unleash your Dream-Mason®.

And some of you, you won't like this. You won't want to play or do the practices. That's fine. But reading this book is only touching the surface of taking on your life at a new level. Doing the work to shift who you are being, through identifying who you have been and taking actions toward creating the life you want, will be the key.

YOUR TURN:

1) What stories and messages did you hear as a child? Come up with at least 5. How do these stories continue to unfold in your present life?

2) Write out your fear story. Describe what happened in detail. If there is more than one coming to you, write them all out. Identify at least 3 things you learned about yourself from them.

3) Make a list of 10 things your story gives you, and 10 things your story costs you.

3 | READY, SET, CHANGE

◆ ◆ ◆

"GET TO THE ISLAND, AND BURN THE BOATS!"

- TONY ROBBINS

Bottom line. *This is it, the startling line to moving forward. This chapter about:*
- *Normalizing the experience of being inspired to change and confronted by what's actually required at the same time*
- *Identifying the number one thing that stops most of us —and breaking it up!*

EVERYONE GETS A BREAKTHROUGH

O kay, so you've had the realization that you want things to change. Now what?

There is a ton of talk about Breakthroughs out in the world today. They are everywhere, breakthroughs in fitness apparel, laundry detergent, technology, and even banking.

Have a breakthrough. Create a breakthrough. "I had a breakthrough and it changed everything."

But what is a breakthrough?

Breakthroughs are realizations, epiphanies, moments of clarity, or new awareness. They aren't change in themselves. However, change, or transformation is a permanent shift that comes not only with new awareness but with actions, behaviors one is creating and/or cultivating.

Let's look at this through my story--I woke up and realized I wasn't a great guy. I wasn't a bad guy, I was just sort of a jerk. I was negative, I was jealous of other people's successes, and I felt entitled to success without the effort. I used women and booze to make myself feel good, without a real care about who I hurt or what dangerous situations I put myself in. I watched roughly 1-4 hours of TV a day, usually late into the night, often to drown out the emptiness, loneliness or inability to be with myself.

When I returned from Costa Rica, I knew I wanted to change my life. I had a simple breakthrough. I knew things had to be different. I could see life wasn't working for me the way it was going. I could see how my patterns, behaviors, attitude and the perspective through which I saw the world was creating this. I knew it had to change.

My starting points were simple. I came up with them myself. I could see where I wasn't flourishing that's where I began to generate changes.

The first change was to my routine. I quit watching tv. I decided to read one book a week. I started taking non-fiction book recommendations, my only requirement being that the subject had to be about learning or growing. I started reading Robert Kiyosaki, Tony Robbins, Og Mandino, and Simon Sinek.

The second change I had to make was in my attitude. I couldn't keep being ungrateful, negative, jealous of others, nor could I hide it all behind the excuse of "being realistic."

What is realistic anyway? You might not like this, but actually it's negative or pessimistic. Think about it, have you ever heard anyone say, "Realistically, this is going to go great!" It's not a thing. We use realistic to dampen and lower our expectations.

I was going to be positive!

No matter what!

At least that was my goal and intention.

Third, I knew that if I was going to generate lasting change, I would have to put more focus into my health and overall well-being. I threw out all of my muscle-building protein powders, my vitamins and supplements. I committed to consuming Whole Food Based Products aka products that are food, not isolated ingredients like vitamins, additives, or chemicals. I cut back on my drinking. I cut back on meats and cheeses and other foods that were fatty and made me feel lazy. Soon my energy levels were up, I was losing weight and I felt great

The last change related to the adage that "you become the median of the five people you spend the most time with."

That means that if you hang out with five assholes, you're likely to become one. If you spend most of your time with five super kind and successful people you are likely on your way to becoming super kind and successful yourself. When I looked around, I knew great people. But most of them, like me, weren't where they wanted to be in life. Most of them were frustrated, drank too much, partied too much, lacked focus, complained a lot, and simply weren't living up to their full potential. I was just like them.

The thing that surprised me was that I didn't have to "break up" with my friends. The ones that my changes upset or those who weren't supportive did it for me. As I started eating better, drinking less, reading more, and being intentionally more positive, a lot of them actually didn't want to be around me. I wasn't getting the phone calls or texts I used to get. I wasn't getting invited to things anymore. I can't say exactly why this happens, my assertion is that when you make changes to improve yourself people who aren't working to improve themselves don't want to be around you as you become a reflection of what they aren't willing or don't want to confront.

With the changes, I started seeking out new friends, new environments to hangout in, and new people with whom to surround myself.

I started going to health workshops and spent more time in bookstores and gyms than in bars. I started calling people whom I knew to be positive, happy, and successful, and started asking them for advice.

In reality, that's it. That's all I did to start. It's all I knew how to do. But I was committed to it and I stuck to it every single day. I was motivated to change. And when you get truly motivated, beyond the feeling, when motivation becomes a calling nothing can stop you.

While I didn't know what I was doing, in the process I learned a ton, read over 100 books, took courses and classes, got paid to support others, and paid to be supported. I have shifted my entire life. From all of that I feel honored to give you more than I had, when I started. And yet, it will still be up to you to create your own path because there is no right path, just your own unique path.

WARNING DANGER AHEAD

Are you ready?

I will warn you...

Some people aren't going to like it.

Some people are going to be threatened.

Some people will accuse you of being unrealistic or trying to be someone you're not.

And it won't be easy. You will naturally slide back to your old, safe, comfortable patterns, even if they weren't working for you.

There will be internal and external anger, ridicule, and possibly isolation.

But know this you are changing and with change comes a readjustment, creating a new normal, a new floor, and a new life. And change doesn't happen without joy, being open, willing, and often struggle or new challenges.

When you start doing positive things for yourself and for your life, people around you will get triggered. Some of them will be supportive to your face and do nothing but talk shit behind your back. Others won't be able to be around you, they'll question your motives, debate if your changes are genuine, or just flat out be dicks about it.

The thing is, the people who are doing great and leading happy, positive lives will support you and love you and cheer you on. But people that aren't will struggle with this because it makes them face their own lack of control and the poor choices they make in their lives.

Before you, they could always blame everything on others, say they didn't have options, blame society, culture, politics, or simply their perceived superiors. Before you they could just be surrounded by others like them so they wouldn't have to feel alone in their unfulfilled, unhappy, unsatisfied lives. By creating change in your life, you unintentionally hold up a mirror for those that want to change but aren't. And that is a difficult thing to be with.

My advice - stick to your guns and be compassionate to with yourself. Let those people do them and love them exactly for who they are and who they aren't. Remember they are on their own path and it's their unique path and isn't supposed to look like yours.

I expected and demanded that I would be uber-positive. I knew that I couldn't let my guard down for one minute, because my auto-negativity and old habits and patters would quickly swoop back in. I didn't have a group to support me or accountability structures. It was just me trying to change 33 years of routine and practice. So, I was looking for the positive and the gold everywhere in my personal and professional life. For some people I was annoying as fuck. To others I was a joke. To a few I was welcomed as a nice change.

At first it was weird, hard and confronting. I would post things on my social media or say things in the office and people would look at me oddly or message me asking if I was okay. I started getting second hand messages from friends asking if I'd found Jesus or had a mental breakdown.

Their surprise made sense, I had been the worst example or representative of the restaurant culture for years. While I was really talented and effective in the industry, having successfully opened roughly 15 restaurants and bars in across more than 6 states, I was also Mr. Negativity. I was a culprit of a past littered with inappropriate relationships, nights spent drunk and even sometimes drunk while working.

But I knew deep in my heart, I was through with that life. It was really and truly over, and I wasn't just saying it. I was beginning to practice it daily.

Eventually, people saw and believed the changes. They will with you also. And you will find the people who get it and support you.

My people were the fellow entrepreneurs in my family. The Life Coaches I kept meeting at different networking events. My parents. The year-long intensive Coach & Leadership Training Program that sky-rocketed my transformation.

It won't start for you like that. It could, but mine happened like that because it was perfect for me. Your way will be your way. You don't have to take a program or read 100 books. You don't have to go to therapy or hire a coach. While I love them, you don't have to bow down to Tony Robbins, Gabby Bernstein or Lewis Howes, but it wouldn't hurt. None of these things hurt. And there are hundreds of other people and structures available. What's important is that you find yours, create your breakthrough and find a way to get out of your comfort zone.

We commit to things we are not prepared mentally or physically ready or able to do.

We quit when the going gets tough, because commitment

for many of us ends when we no longer "feel like it".

Those feelings are often influenced by the people around us, and inherently the people around us are challenged when we commit to change.

So, what will keep us committed? What will hold us to the changes we crave when our feelings or the people around us confront our new behaviors, beliefs, and goals.

YOUR TURN:

1) Notice what came up for you when you read the section about how not everyone will support you as you change.

2) Are you willing to decide right now that you won't let however it felt stop you from pursuing the change you desire?

3) When you have quit in the past, what were the stories, ideas, or reasons you gave for quitting? Identify them now, so as to not allow them to stop you this time around.

4 | THE BASIC PILLARS OF CHANGE

"Your life does not get better by chance, it gets better by change."

- JIM ROHN

Bottom Line. *There are two basic pillars of change:*
- *Foundation*
- *Beams of Support*

FOUNDATION

The first pillar, Foundation, is made up of the following aspects:

- **The Goal aka Where are You Going?** A goal or outcome so to speak. If we called an Uber or Lyft, they wouldn't take us anywhere if we didn't give them an exact address. We couldn't just say, "oh, take us somewhere over there." You cannot get somewhere if you don't know where you are going! Where do you want to go? What is the desired outcome? What is your goal?

- **Your North Star aka Your Commitments.** What are you actually committed to? Not just for the goal, but in life? Are you committed to family, health, love, adventure, fun, God...or what? Are you willing to be committed to the outcome you choose and the future you want to create and the person it's going to take to make that goal a reality?

- **Your Oath aka Your Mission & Values.** Who do you want to be in this journey on your path towards your Commitments? Who is the person you want to be thought of as? What is the way you want your goal, product or company to be viewed or the things you want it to stand for?

- **Visualization. Visualize it.** Seriously, can you see it in your mind? Can you see the things you want, the life you want, in your mind's eye? You need to!

- **What For.** Why do you want what you want? Why do you care? People often say, "I want to make more money." Great, why? What will the money get you? They say, "more travel and more stuff and less debt." Ok, great. But what for? What will doing that or getting those things give you?

- **Well-being.** It's bigger than just "your health". If you aren't healthy you have nothing. The old saying goes, people who are healthy have lots of dreams, the person that isn't healthy has one. And your wellbeing is a culmination of health, mindset, relationship, financial, spiritual, mental, sexual, and other aspects of your life.

- **The Holy Grail aka Loving Yourself.** It's everything. If you don't love yourself there will always be something missing. No matter how much money you earn. How much stuff you have. How hot your partner is and what great things people say about you. How many promotions or houses you have or vacations you take. If you don't love yourself there will be a massive gap in your life.

BEAMS OF SUPPORT

The second pillar, Beams of Support, includes the following aspects:

- **Mindfulness.** Your mind is naturally in a state of "Monkey Mind" as the Buddhists say. It's reacting, responding, worrying, and thinking about the past and the future and rarely stops just to be present. To create a balanced, fulfilled and pleasurable life one must be able to be present.

- **Routine.** Everything in life is a rhythm, the ocean flows in and out. The sun sets and rises. Our lungs expand and contract. Nature blooms and dies. Everything has a rhythm. The only way you will create the life you want, as well as accomplish the audacious goals you have, will be through consistency which can be created through routine.

- **Integrity.** This isn't about morals. It's about personal integrity. Being the person you say you will be. Doing the things you say you will do. Letting your actions and being stay in alignment with who you say you are. If you don't have personal integrity, you likely will let yourself down.

- **Structures of Success.** These are the ways you will set yourself up to succeed. This includes planning, accountability, ways to measure accountability, reward systems, personal reinforcement, and anything else that supports you around all the things above.

Now we are going to take some time to move through each of these in the following chapters. We will create practices so you can do the work to get you moving forward. You can go step by step through each pillar or you can read this whole book first and come back. Listen to what you need and what you think best supports your goals.

5 | GREATNESS, IT STARTS WITH A GOAL

◆ ◆ ◆

"A goal is not always meant to be reached, it often serves simply as somethings to aim at."

- BRUCE LEE

Bottom line. *Set a goal before you move forward. This chapter is about:*
- *Understanding all of the aspects that make up a powerful goal*
- *Setting a goal, woohoo!*

THE GOAL AKA
"WHERE ARE YOU GOING?"

If we were running a marathon, we would all know where the finish line is. There would be no questions or doubts about it. It would be a clearly marked and measurable destination that any objective observer would be able to identify.

What would it be like to run a marathon if the finish line wasn't clearly defined? Imagine if it kept moving and as you ran you never knew where it was going to be, which way to go, or even how much further it was to get there. There may be some people who love this kind of challenge. But for most people, you'd have to be crazy to sign up for that.

For most of us, however, this is how we run our lives and create our goals. We aren't objective. We aren't specific and detailed. We leave a lot of open-ended questions and use circumstances as an excuse to avoid measuring our success because we don't know what exactly to measure or how to measure it.

This makes reaching our goals that much harder!

Stop doing it!

Right now, think of a huge goal you have. Anything. Huge!

Now go big.

Even bigger.

This is a big, audacious goal, something you are afraid you couldn't even accomplish.

Got it?

Perfect.

Take a very deep breath. Let out all the anxiety you just created. Do that again. This time breath in slowly to a count of four, then hold it while you count to four, then release it slowly as you also count to four. Do that again, two more times.

Awesome.

Now let's start defining your goals.

First, by when do you declare you will achieve this goal? I'm looking for an exact date, not like Summer 2021. Exact, like May 5, 2020.

Got it?

Or did you get scared? Are you finding reasons that this won't work for you and your idea?

Put that bullshit down *right now*.

If JFK could declare in front of the world that we would put a man on the Moon in the current decade of the time, you can make a declaration to yourself, even though you don't know *how*.

JFK and NASA didn't know how either.

But everything starts with a declaration. A destination. A goal. Without that you're just floating and hoping.

If we go back to our marathon analogy, a lot of people that run their first marathons don't know how, but they accept the date of the scheduled marathon as their goal.

Ready to do that now? It's just practice, there is no punishment. Pick something you are working on, something big.

Now you don't want the measurement to be ambiguous, you want it to be crystal clear to even someone who isn't paying attention. Everyone knows where the marathon finish line is, it's not up to one runner to decide, and it doesn't move. If it's not crystal clear to an objective observer than it leaves you wiggle room to get out of your commitment or suddenly decide you accomplished it, even if by massaging the goal.

For instance, if my goal is around my business, I might say something like I will reach 2 Million Dollars in net sales by August 23, 2020.

If my goal was around relationships, I might say something like I will be 100% moved in and living with my partner in a house by May 6, 2020.

So, what is your date? By what date will your goal be complete?

Maybe your goal is a feeling. You want to be more satisfied or happy. Now you get to be creative. So, if you were more satisfied or happier. What would that look like? What might you be doing that you aren't doing now?

As an example, if I was happier, I would be hiking at least once a week. I would be going out socially with friends at least 1-2 times a week. I would be watching less than 4 hours of TV per week. I would be taking a vacation at least 3 times a year for at least 7 days each. You could go on and on here. The point is, if you were happier you would be behaving and living differently. So, what would an objective person see?

How will you measure if you reached your goal?

Nice work! You have a goal, with a measurable outcome. That's awesome. Most people when setting goals refuse to do this because it makes it very real. Their brains or their ego tell them it's not a good idea and will create all of the reasons and circumstances to make it seem like it's a great idea to avoid it.

But that won't be you! You have a goal. You have a place you are working to get to. And you have the courage to get out of your comfort zone.

Well Done!

YOUR TURN:

1) Come up with your goal, make it specific and measurable.

2) Decide by what date you will have met your goal.

3) Write down the goal and the date. Post it somewhere, specifically somewhere you will see it often. Bonus points if it's a space where other people will see it too.

6 | COMMITMENT, YOUR NORTH STAR

◆ ◆ ◆

"Commitment is what turns a promise into reality."

- ABRAHAM LINCOLN

Bottom line. *You are about to get super clear on your commitments. This chapter is about:*
- *Aligning our commitments with what really matters to us*
- *Learning to embrace commitment as empowering and freeing*

YOUR NORTH STAR

What does commitment mean to you?

How might you define it?

Seriously, I want you to take a minute...or two or maybe five as it's kind of a big deal and think about it.

Do you make commitments? When? Where? What is required for you to make one?

Do you stick to them? No matter what? Or just until the circumstances are juicy or hard enough that you get to quit?

Do you avoid them? When you think about commitments what comes up for you?

Here's another way to think about commitment. If commitment was an actual man or a woman you were dating, I know, it's weird, but seriously, if commitment were a person, how might you describe your relationship to them?

It might look something like this:

I overcommit, I say I'm going to do things and then I have to many things on my plate, so I don't do them.

I make promises and don't always keep them, but always have a reason or excuse so it seems reasonable that I didn't do what said I was going to do.

I complete my commitments when it comes to easy things, like reading a book, a workout or watching all the seasons of Game of Thrones. But when it comes to big things like relationships, writing a book, opening that business I want to start or other things I can be less reliable to complete them.

Why ask all these questions about commitment?

Because commitment is the only thing separating you from everything you ever wanted in your life! Well, choosing to commit and choosing it over and over again, is the only thing separating you from everything you have ever wanted in your life!

So, it's kind of a big deal.

Tony Robbins says,

> *"I believe life is constantly testing us for our level of commitment, and life's greatest rewards are reserved for those who demonstrate a never-ending commitment to act until they achieve. This level of resolve can move mountains, but it must be constant and consistent. As simplistic as this may sound, it is still the common denominator separating those who live their dreams from those who live in regret."*

We might simply say, if you aren't living your dreams, it's either because you haven't made a committed choice in declaring what your dreams are, or you have not been committed to the actions that it takes to generate them. Regardless, it's your commitment that's out. And look there are some of you that are going to say, "no, some people aren't living their dreams because: they don't have money, their ideas suck, they don't have support, they don't know what they want, etc…"

Consider that if they were committed enough to a goal, like a deep-in-their-bones commitment, they could create support, generate money or even succeed with a crappy idea… the pet rock, Furbies, fidget spinners…

And for those of you saying, "but I would be committed, if just I knew what I wanted." Be willing or committed to give up the idea or the story that you don't know what you want. This might create the space for purpose or passion to show up.

Frankly, I don't buy the "I don't know what I want," "I don't have a passion or a purpose," or the "I don't have any dreams."

Yes, you *fucking* do!

There was never a kid who didn't have a dream. There was never a kid who didn't dream what it would be like to do something. There was never a kid who didn't enjoy or love doing *something*. And there was never a kid who wasn't creative or didn't have an imagination.

We simply forget we are those kids.

We forgot, hid, ignored these dreams, passions, and love. We were convinced they weren't plausible by our culture, our families, our friends, our schools, our churches, our governments and everyone else. We were told we weren't good enough, that it's too hard, that it takes money or time, or you have to know someone. We were told that we can only do it if we are white or black or skinny or fat. We were told... blah blah blah blah blah.

We all had dreams.

We all had passions.

We all had imaginations and creative genius inside of us.

If you are one of those people that believe they can't, or they don't know how, or they don't have a passion or a purpose, commit to breaking that sad fucking story. Commit to discovering your passion. To reawakening your creativity. To generating a spark inside of you that creates purpose in your life.

How?

Choose that commitment!

There are classes on all of these things. There are people to talk to, books to read, surveys to take. There are opportunities everywhere. If you're committed to changing your life, committed to shifting something, committed to living differently than you are now, there is nothing that can stop you!

So, let's talk about creating or crafting commitments.

We are nothing without our commitments. Imagine deciding to go grocery shopping and half way there you decide to go to the gym instead. So, you go to the gym, and while you work out you are on your phone the whole time, and you leave straight for the bar without a shower. You walk up to the bar and decide you don't like the look of the people there, so you leave to get coffee instead. So, you walk inside the coffee shop, and leave after 5 minutes because you were unwilling to decide what you wanted to order. You go home and don't eat dinner because you're not sure what you want to eat, and then you flip channels on the tv until you fall asleep.

While there is nothing inherently wrong with this life, my guess is this life would be vastly unfulfilling. While I don't think most of us are living this extreme example, maybe something in this story resonated with you. The point was to clarify that we already are operating within commitments all over our lives. We choose our commitments and then we choose the actions that support those commitments.

We brush our teeth daily, almost on auto-pilot which makes me believe we are committed to having clean breath, teeth that aren't rotting and good oral hygiene. We do things like make it to the gym, get to the yoga class, make plans with friends, or take vacations. We get to work daily, go on dates, get married, have kids and some of us hit a lot of our goals or milestones. I believe all the things we do routinely and the bigger decisions we make are related to our deeper values and commitments.

When we get married, we make a verbal commitment, and sign a contract. When we agree to friends to meet for dinner, we are committing to that social arrangement. When we take a job, we commit to complete the job requirements and duties and the employer commits to pay us. I'm not going to go on and on, but we are already in commitments all over our lives. Some of us realize it and own the responsibility that comes with a commitment and some of us…not so much.

But I want you to think about commitment bigger than you have ever thought about it before.

It's sort of a weird questions to pose. What are you committed to?

I'm committed to Ease, Authenticity, Play, Well-being and Inspiration. When I get stuck in life, this is where I look. I look to my commitments and ask from Ease, Authenticity, Play, Well-being and Inspiration what might I do? How might I do what I was doing differently?

I like to think of my commitments as my North Star. A guiding light that I can always find and turn to, to support my journey.

Your North Star can be anything. It could be love, peace, joy, celebration, adventure, courage, passion or a million and one other things. Look big.

For instance, if you said,

"I'm committed to family and friends," I would say you are committed to love or maybe to relationship.

If you said, "I'm committed to yoga and being healthy," I would say you are actually committed to your well-being.

If you said, "I'm committed to having fun, spending time with my kids doing activities, going on dates and enjoying my life." I might say you are committed to adventure or play.

What I'm pointing to is it's bigger than the actual content things you are likely thinking about.

Imagine you could clean the slate of your life. You get a fresh start. You right now, get to hit the reset button on your life, even if only for this moment and start again.

So, from this blank slate, what kind of person do you want to be?

What kind of life do you want to live?

How do you want others to speak about you? Relate to you? And hold you?

How do you want to want to relate to yourself?

How do you want to be thought of after you pass?

So, go big, what are you committed to on a large scale?

I am committed to (BLANK)

There is no right amount. Shoot to find 3-5 things you know you are 100% committed to.

Did you do it?

If so, nice job.

If not, go back. Do it!

Side note. For many of you this is new. As you go through the book you might get more specific or just more clearly realize what you are committed to. If that's the case, no worries, you can change it or adjust it.

Now, take your North Star, your commitment list, and post it somewhere that you can see it daily.

This is a great practice. You aren't practiced in focusing on these things so likely after you walk away you will forget about them and go back to your default setting. Let's break that up by posting them in places you CAN see them. I have my commitments posted on my phone's background, my laptop screen, a post-it on the bathroom mirror, and on my desk.

Where will you post yours?

There is one last thing we need to touch on before we move on.

Commitment exists outside of the circumstances that arise.

Read that line again.

Often, we have commitments and then we break them due to circumstances that arise. That's not a commitment. A commitment is something we do despite or in-spite of circumstances.

That is commitment. Commitment is not stopping and not quitting. Commitment is declaring you will do, be or create something and make it happen.

Does that mean commitments are forever? No. I don't believe that. Let's say you were in a horrible marriage. You sought help, went to counseling, used legal actions or did whatever you could do to improve or change the situation because despite the circumstances you were deeply committed to the person or the marriage. You could decide to leave the commitment, because you have a higher commitment to well-being, or kindness, love or self-respect.

While my highest commitments are Ease, Authenticity, Play, Well-being and Inspiration, sometimes I realize I must choose to reinvent another commitment to have it fall in line with my higher commitments. My commitment to play might run into my commitment of wellbeing. How can I create both? We can alter our relationships to things to have them fit into our commitments. At other times we have to look to our higher commitments.

Sometimes I think of my highest commitments like this:

If I had a sick and potentially fatally ill child, how far would I go to help them? Where would I stop? How far would I go to get them help? And even when I had tried everything in my power and exhausted every option, even then would I keep trying?

I simply wouldn't quit! I would keep going and going and going until I found a way to help them or until they were taken from me. That being said, I would be doing all that from my highest commitments.

What if you brought that type of commitment and rigor to everything else you do? What if you weren't willing to stop when you heard no or weren't willing to slow down because you were tired or "didn't feel like it". What if it didn't matter what other people thought, what the weather was or any other circumstance. What if you just kept going until you produced the results you wanted in more aspects of your life?

What would you be capable of? What would you produce? What would your life look like?

"The power to make and keep commitments to ourselves is the essence of developing the basic habits of effectiveness."

- STEPHEN COVEY

YOUR TURN:

1) What is your current relationship to commitments? Journal about it.

2) If you could wipe the slate clean, what would you be committed to starting today? Come up with 3-5 things.

3) Post those new commitments somewhere you will see them often.

7 | YOUR OATH

◆ ◆ ◆

"A small body of determined spirits fired by an unquenchable faith in their mission can alter the course of history."

- MAHATMA GANDHI

Bottom line. *This chapter is about:*
- *Understanding and creating our personal mission and values*
- *Creating an oath so powerful it moves everything forward*

YOUR MISSION AND VALUES

So, you have what you are committed to, your North Star. Now, let's build and add on to this. When the United States was formed, we know the Founding Fathers wanted to create a democratic country, but what did that actually mean? A Democracy was their North Star, it's where they were headed, but what did that look like? What was the "Mission" in getting there and what were the "Values" that would lead to success or support the goal?

Stephen Covey might have been the first to say that not only do businesses need a set of Mission and Values, but we as individuals also need them if we want to lead fulfilling and successful lives.

Who do you want to be?

For example, I want to be powerful, strong, vulnerable, kind, loving, fun, playful, determined, honorable, confident, adventure, and compassionate.

When you think about the person you want to be in the future, how would you describe that person? What does that person do and create? How do they act? Who are they being when they do all those things? (Example: Strong, Leader, Writer, Speaker, Honorable, Playful)

When you think about the things the person you want to be does and how they behave what words might you use to describe that? (Example: Integrity, Heart, Passion, Poised, Creative)

When you think about the things you want to accomplish in your life, not the small tasks but the larger impact you want to have, how would you describe that? (Example: Love, Inspiration, Joy, Adventure, Leader, Relentless)

My answers are:

I want to be a strong, vulnerable leader, a man of integrity, a human who comes from his heart. I want to be a man who is his word, follows through on his actions and leaves the world a better, more inspired and positive place than the way he found it. Through this journey, I want to be love, authenticity, play, warrior, light and radiance.

Now if you didn't already answer the questions above go back and do that.

Look at what you wrote. Let's distill it into a mission statement. A mission statement is in short, a summary of your goals, aims, and values.

For me it looks like this:

My mission is to support every human in unleashing their inner DreamMason®, knowing they are whole, capable and courageous enough to look within to express the vision that radiates from their hearts and brave enough to take the actions to make it a reality.

Now look at what you wrote and distill it into your personal values.

Mine are:
- Come from heart, love, understanding, and acceptance
- Be bold and a powerful stand for greatness
- Integrity
- Compassion
- Vulnerability & Authenticity
- Be committed to developing and growing myself
- Fun & Play
- Be in service of others
- Don't be attached to others' results

- Be a lighthouse

Now it's your turn. Go for it. You can't get this wrong.

Awesome job! Now you have a North Star as well as Mission and Values.

Now the key is to start practicing living into these things. Nobody says this will be easy, it will require commitment, practice and lots of getting up and trying again after you mess up.

A practice for you is to print these out and post them every-where, on your phone, computer, mirrors, on walls, doors, everywhere. Put them everywhere until you know and feel them in your bones.

By when will you have these words posted everywhere?

Make it happen!

YOUR TURN:

1) Define your Mission.

2) Define your Personal Values.

3) Post both your Mission and your Values.

8 | BACK TO THE FUTURE

◆ ◆ ◆

"Your future hasn't been written yet. No one's has. Your future is whatever you make it. So make it a good one."

- DOC BROWN, BACK TO THE FUTURE

Bottom line. *There is power in visualization. This chapter is about:*
· *Harnessing the power of our minds to create the imprint for the visions we are creating*

VISUALIZATION

Visualize it! We hear this from great athletes all the time. Science has even proven the power of visualization leads to greater percentages of success. So, now it's your turn to start visualizing your life.

BACK TO THE FUTURE –
THE EXERCISE

One of my favorite exercises I do myself and with my clients is writing the future. It's actually pretty simple and it's fun, which is the best part.

Nothing we as humans have ever created exists if it first wasn't imagined or created in the mind. Nothing. Someone thought about going to the Moon far before it happened. Steve Jobs thought of the iPod and iPhone far before Apple actually created them.

If you're working through this book and doing the exercises and tools, I encourage you to pull out a new blank sheet of paper for this exercise. You can also type it if you prefer.

Let's get right to it. I want you to take a few minutes and find a quiet private place to sit. Close your eyes and take a few very intentional deep breaths in through your nose and out through your mouth.

When you breathe in think about, and breathe in, possibility and universal energy. When you breathe out, let everything go.

After a few rounds go back to normal breathing and start thinking about your life 1 year, or 20, 30, 40, 50 or even 60 years from now. I actually like to do this exercise in two ways. The first is picturing 1 year from now, the other is from the end of my life. Let's start with the 1 year from now.

So, you are imagining your life 1 year from today. I really want you to get present to who you *want to be* a year from now. Where are you? What have you created, built or produced? Do you look different? The same? What about your clothes and environment? Who is around you? What are you doing for work? How is your attitude and energy?

Sometimes when doing this people have specifics in mind. For example, they know that a year from now, they want to have their movie script written, have lost 20 pounds, have found a loving partner, moved, ended a relationship, got a new job or something else. Whatever it is, take a few minutes to imagine it. When you feel you can see what your life looks like open your eyes and start writing a letter from Future You to Present You. To make it easy, just start with,

Dear Shelly, this sounds crazy but it's you, it's Shelly from the future and I want to tell you what life is like, what you've created, how you feel, what you've accomplished and been up to over the last...

In this letter make sure you really dig into what you've done, who you had to be to do that. What feelings are associated with it. What has changed as a result of what you have accomplished. What might be next for you.

Do your best to write about one full page. This should be fun, exciting. It's almost like you are writing a blueprint or a movie script for your life. Enjoy it.

Another option is the life version, which means, picturing yourself near the end of your life. Choose, how old will you be when you die? Take a guess. Imagine yourself there at that age. Where are you? Who's around you? What are they saying? Doing? What are your relationships like? What have you accomplished, done and who have you been in your

life?
From that place write yourself a letter from the end, telling yourself about the experience of your life.

Again, have fun. These exercises are intended to get you present to your imagination of the future that you'd really love to have and the life you'd like to create.

After you write it. Put it down. Walk away. Leave it. Let the Universe take it. You just planted a seed.

YOUR TURN:

1) Complete the Back to the Future Exercise.

2) Or notice why you are resistant to completing the Back to the Future Exercise.

9 | WHY DO WE EVEN CARE?

$$\blacklozenge \; \blacklozenge \; \blacklozenge$$

"WHY is not about making money. That's a result. It's a purpose, cause or belief. It's the very reason (you) your organization exists."

– SIMON SINEK

Bottom line. *This chapter is about:*
- *Generating our What For, or our Why*
- *Getting crystal clear on what's behind what we want*

WHAT FOR:
YOUR GOAL'S HEARTBEAT

Sometimes it may seem like the magic question is why? Why are you even going for the goal you're going for? Why do you so desperately want to start that business, write that book, get in shape, find a partner, have kids, make a million dollars, or buy that dream house?

Seriously, Why?

Going after your dreams is a lot of work. Creating the life you want can be hard, it can be a road filled with heart break, challenges, obstacles, stress, long days and no sleep. Falling in love, creating an amazing relationship takes work, focus, commitment and a willingness to get your heart broken.

I don't say this to dissuade you from what you want or going after your goal but to have you get focused on why you want it. Consider you want to make a million dollars. For some people this is the goal or dream. But a million dollars is just a lot of numbers on a screen or tons of green pieces of paper. In reality that's it.

What I know is it's not about the million dollars, it's about something you think the million dollars will get you. Maybe it's a car or house or lifestyle. Maybe it's comfort or peace or out of debt. Regardless, when you have the car, house lifestyle, are out of debt what will you then have?

Maybe it's back to comfort, joy, peace or security...whatever it is, that's what you actually want!
Get clear on what you want, because so many people are thinking of something that isn't what they actually want, and then when they get the money or whatever, they are still unfulfilled.

Why is having a Why so important? Because if you don't have a powerful What For or Why, what will keep you moving forward when you "don't wanna," when you hit an obstacle, when the person you loves doesn't support you, when circumstances change and make your goal more difficult? What will keep you going when you don't feel good or just don't feel like it? What will keep you going when your motivation runs out and whatever inspired you to start is far in the past?

Your "What For" is your goal's Heartbeat. It's the piece that keeps the whole thing moving forward. Without a "What For" it is predictable and likely that at some point you will simply run out of the inspiration, motivation, flow or whatever other temporary fuel you are running on. If your "What For" is big enough or powerful enough it has the ability to keep you going when you otherwise would stop.

So how do we create that Heartbeat...Your "What For"?

I believe some of us think we know why: our kids, our goals, we want to, we have to, we need money, we want a boat or a house, we want to be able to retire or just we just want abs cause they look good. It's not for me to decide why you want anything, this is a personal choice. But what is important is for you to take a look deeper.

As I said before your likely first answer probably isn't what you actually want. For instance, what is my What For in writing this book? I am committed to impacting people's lives through connection, through inspiration and through authenticity. I also love to write.

While I feel it's my purpose to generate Joy in my life and support others in learning to do the same, I believe it's my passion to write. So, in bringing the two together I found a basic "What For". But this is still on the surface.

If I look deeper, I am writing this book because if I don't, I will forever feel like I left something on the table. I will feel that I didn't give it 100%. If I don't write this book, I will have simply started another thing I didn't finish, a pattern with which I am all too familiar.

So, when I think I don't want to write the next word, page or chapter I remind myself that it's time to start finishing things. It's time to finish what I started because I said so, because I made a commitment to it, because I said so.

Let's write down your goals and take a look at your What For's.

I like to advise my clients on having 3 or 4 goals when they start working with me. It's a good number of things you can be working on while not becoming too pressured or distracted.

I don't think it's beneficial when my clients have only 1 or 2 goals. It's like putting all their eggs in a basket or two, and when they hit the circumstances, obstacles, or challenges that life will throw at them sometimes they get discouraged. When you have 3 or 4 goals, some are moving powerfully forward and others aren't, so you have things to focus on when you are stuck on others.

YOUR TURN:

1) Define your "What For" for the goal you came up with.

2) Write out your Why or What For and powerfully share it with 3 people.

10 | YOUR BEDROCK

◆ ◆ ◆

"The first wealth is health."

- RALPH WALDO EMERSON

Bottom line. *Without health, all your goals become impossible. This chapter is about:*
· *Realizing just how expansive our well-being is*
· *Creating strong well-being practices*

WELL-BEING

A KA health, self-care, taking care of yourself, whatever you want to call it.

If Well-being isn't in place, you're building your dreams on quick sand!

My Uncle says, and I'm sure he stole this from someone, "a person who has their health has a million dreams, but a person who doesn't have their health has but one dream."

Now I wish Well-being was as simple as your health. Consider that your Well-being is vastly more profound than your health. If your health was the earth, your well-being is the universe.

Well-being is critical because without it there is nothing else. If you are sick, if you are tired, if your stress levels are off the charts, if you don't have healthy relationships with others, if your sex life isn't healthy, if you don't know how to let go and relax or don't have some sort of spiritual connection, then here is an opportunity to take a powerful look at your well-being.

Let's think of well-being as the ground floor of the sky scraper of a life you're creating or remodeling. If the foundation isn't solid who cares what the 56th floor looks like as it will soon be crumbling down.

If you're sitting there rolling your eyes and saying to yourself, I didn't buy this book to be told how to be healthy or to find God. That's okay, but if you're reading this book, there is likely something missing or off about your life that you're looking to change and how would you know if this is it if you aren't willing to take a look at it.

The best part about well-being is you get to create your own standards for it. For instance, my sense of excellent well-being isn't close to what another's might be.

I ask my clients to look in all the corners of their life to see what's getting their attention. Imagine if you were perfectly healthy, had great a relationship, a job you loved, a wonderful connection to spirit, but you worry about money daily, and maybe you don't sleep well because of it. Maybe it's a source of tension in your life. Your well-being is compromised because your relationship with money is not in a healthy place.

So, let's take a Well-being Inventory and give each area a grade of A through F, A obviously being the best. Rank your well-being in the following areas:

Diet
Exercise
Marriage/Partner
Spirituality
Sexual
Financial
Social
Work
Family
Sleep
Environment
Mental
Recreation
Emotional

So, what do you notice?

Where did you rank yourself a C or below?

Where are you strongest and ranked yourself an A or B?

If you look at the areas where you are the most out of alignment, below a C, and you wanted to start building those up, what might be something you could practice doing every day, that you would like to be doing every day?

Let's create a list of practices that you could do daily that would start to grow, support, and enhance your well-being.

When I say practices, what I mean is let's create things, activities, habits, or things you will do that you will try and do on a daily basis. And these are things that if we don't do, we are not going beat ourselves up about. Literally like we are practicing, not judging, or evaluating.

In baseball, players go to batting practice, the whole purpose is to simply practice so they are more prepared. It's an exercise. In yoga, it's called a practice as you are always practicing and there is no destination or way to become the best or finish yoga. There's no score card, no grading sheet, no good or bad.

Now let's come up with at least 1-2 daily practices for the areas that fall below a C. You can also create practices for those above a C but consider that those muscles are already strong, and you already know how to do that, so maybe it's time to work some weaker muscles.

For instance, let's say that you rated yourself a D in mental, maybe you could take on a practice of 15 minutes of daily reading, or doing the NY Times Crossword puzzle.

If you rated yourself a F in Environment maybe you could buy or pick fresh flowers weekly and have them in your home, or you could decorate your office work space, so you enjoy being there. Maybe you clean up around the house daily, so your home is tidier.

If you rated yourself low in sleep, maybe you create a bedtime practice or sleep routine and practice waking up and going to bed at a certain time.

If you rated yourself a C or below in spiritual, maybe you could start meditating daily, or doing yoga or simply reading spirituality-based books and expanding that area of your life.

Practices don't have to be complex or hard. I had a client that created a practice of doing a gratitude journal with her 5-year-old daughter every night before bed. It was a genius idea and not only a way for her to work on her relationship with gratitude and joy but also to teach her daughter a valuable practice while spending some quality time together.

I had another client create a practice of giving his phone to his wife when he got home from work. She would hide it and give it back to him in the morning as he wanted to be more present with his kids and he was addicted to looking at his phone. Over time after he broke the habit, he was able to simply put it down and didn't have the impulse to check it all the time.

There are no right or wrong practices. If a practice doesn't seem to work or isn't supporting the life you want to be creating, toss it and try another. But notice if you're simply tossing practices because they are difficult or challenging you and it makes you uncomfortable, or actually because they aren't effective.

You can ask yourself, are they supporting the person you want to be and the life you want to create?

Did you write down your practices?

YOUR TURN:

1) If you have not already, give yourself a grade for all the parts of your Well-Being.

2) Create daily practices for any part of your Well-Being that you ranked a C or lower.

3) Post your well-being practices somewhere that will remind you take them on.

11 | THE HOLY GRAIL

◆ ◆ ◆

"Owning our story and loving ourselves through that process is the bravest thing that we'll ever do."

- BRENE BROWN

Bottom line. *This chapter is about:*
- *Understanding the process of falling in love with ourselves*
- *Noticing the voices in our minds*

LOVING YOURSELF

Y ou can achieve all the success in the world and if you don't love yourself you will need more, want more and never stop. The thing about loving yourself is it makes everything else possible. I'm not saying you can't be successful without loving yourself, but it will be worthless because you will always feel unfulfilled or unsatisfied. When you learn to truly love yourself, everything you do will become frosting on the cake.

Self-love is an ongoing, everyday practice. While everything you are doing will improve and shift the way you related to yourself, you also need to be focused on actually loving yourself. This can be done in various ways. The first is noticing the conversation you are having in your head with yourself. The key word here is *notice*, the conversation and the tone.

I like to refer to this as "The Voices in our Monkey Minds."

"Your mind is a dream where a thousand people talk at the same time, and nobody understands each other. This is the condition of the human mind - a big mitote, (pronounced MIH-TOE-TAY - From Toltecs meaning your mind is a fog) and with that big mitote you cannot see what you really are."

- DON MIGUEL RUIZ

There are tons of voices in our heads. And that can get complex, so I like to say there are three basic voices in our head.

#1 The Hater: You know it, that voice that tells you: you can't, you're not good enough, you failed, you suck, you're too fat, too skinny, not pretty enough, not smart enough, weak, stupid, sick or worthless.

#2 The Wimp: Our inner victim, which is the part of us that gets bullied by The Hater and life. It can't stop thinking about how things should be, shouldn't be, how we could have done it different or better. It obsesses about the past, the fears of the future and anything The Hater slings at it.

#3 The Cheerleader: Cheers whether winning or losing. It acts like it's our friend and tries to protect us because honestly it believes we are safer where we are. Sometimes our only real friend, and often it is the quietest. But at other times, it's our Cheerleader that is actually telling us to eat another scoop of ice cream, or sleep in and don't go to the gym because we deserve to rest. The Cheerleader is the voice that tells us we can, it's happy and inspires us and supports us to keep going and push when we might otherwise quit.

It reminds us to get out of bed and go to the gym. It reminds us to send the text to that loved one because it could make their day. It tries it's best to support us, but it also secretly tries it's best to keep us exactly where we are.

Well, that actually is the thing about all these voices, their main job is to keep us safe. To keep us in our comfort zones, too have us stick with the things that are familiar. They work together or separately to achieve that goal. The mission is to keep us safe, secure and exactly where we are, even if where we are sucks!

I want it to be clear that I'm simplifying the voices in our head. I would assert we have many more, but at the root there are the three with which we are most actively engaged. And frankly these voices served a purpose through evolution. If we were relaxed, felt safe and our minds were tranquil we likely wouldn't have noticed the tiger that was going to spring from the trees or we might not have gathered enough food for a long winter.

Regardless, unless we live in a war-torn country, most of us are relatively safe and not in immediate danger. These voices are the causes for most of our fears, anxieties, stress, don't go after what we really want, never get in touch with our true nature or power, and simply the reason we give up on our dreams,

I believe if you can notice the voices in your head you can see and be fully aware that they are working to keep you stuck. They are just thoughts and not the truth. Most of what they throw at you are stories, interpretations, and not reality. When you become aware of this, you can take power back over your thoughts and fall in love with yourself.

These voices support you living an autopilot-driven existence. You think you are choosing, but in reality, you are responding and reacting to the voices, circumstances and patterns in your life and not what is actually happening. Your Auto-Pilot is your automatic reaction, your default response. You can see it in the way you snap at your partner or your parents when they are on your nerves. How you get when work is piling up. How you act, behave and respond with all the stress of a big trip you might be taking.

Consider that most of the time, roughly 90% your autopilot is running your life. And it's fine, it's probably doing an okay job keeping it all going. But it's not letting you live "your best life" because that is only possible if you can get out of your comfort zone and that is only available if you lower the volume of the negative voices and shut off the autopilot.

Now let's take a deeper look at the three main voices that make up the autopilot.

THE HATER

Aka, the Judge and The Assessor and frankly the fucking prick within us. For all of us the experience of The Hater is different, but what's similar is it's consistently judging us, others, every situation, and everything. Maybe it's a perfectionist or super fearful or trying to control everything. It is always, without fail, looking at how things "should be," or "could be."

The thing is when it comes to The Hater we can never win. The hater was formed as we grew up, we learned "rules about life" or "how life is" from our parents, our experiences, our communities, our churches, and the media. The Hater grew from an early age to use all these things as a prison of programming which rule our life.

> *"There is something in our minds that judges everybody and everything, including the weather, the dog, the cat - everything...we do and don't do, everything we think and don't think, and everything we feel and don't feel. Everything lives under tyranny... many times a day, day after day, for all the years of our lives."*

- DON MIGUEL RUIZ

If we go against The Hater, we subconsciously punish ourselves, we feel guilty, scared, terrified, shameful, embarrassed, stressed and anxious. And when we start interpreting those thoughts through the filter of The Hater, we start hearing The Wimp.

THE WIMP

Aka, the Victim. I believe we all know the victim all too well. Some of us love our victim. Our victim allows us to ignore taking responsibility for our lives, to blame others, to make excuses, to use circumstances and other people as a reason we are not living our life the way we want to. Some of us even pick fights or mess things up purposely so others can subconsciously play the role of The Hater so we can embody The Wimp.

Think about the voice of The Wimp. It tells us we can't, we should stop our workout because we can't push anymore. It tells us we shouldn't start that business because we aren't smart enough, or because the economy isn't good enough. The Wimp convinces us that the girl or a guy won't like us because we don't make enough money or aren't are pretty or handsome enough.

The Wimp says it's not our fault we got fired, it's because we are too old, or the client is a jerk. It tells us it's the government's fault we are broke, or it's because of the Conservatives, Liberals, or even our families. Or maybe it's God's fault.

THE CHEERLEADER

Aka our so-called friend. The Cheerleader just wants us to be safe and comfortable. However, its perception of safety and comfort is an illusion. It thinks eating that extra cookie is a good idea because in the moment it feels good or we deserve it. It thinks skipping that 5am yoga class is self-love and kindness because you "need" a few extra hours of sleep. It believes staying in a bad relationship is being committed to love because it so fears being single again. It's the voice that tells you, you should see a therapist then quickly also tells you, you can't because you can't afford it.

So how do we quiet these voices, empower our values, commitments, and North Star?

The answer starts with The Beams of Support, the second Basic Pillar of Change. The second pillar is designed to empower and support the first pillar.

YOUR TURN:

1) Start noticing when you are on Auto-Pilot. When you notice it, practice being intentional again.

2) Give names to your Hater, Wimp, and Cheerleader.

3) Make a list of which scenarios drive up or trigger your Hater, Wimp, and Cheerleader.

12 | THE MONKEY TAMER

◆ ◆ ◆

"The ego is like a clever monkey, which can co-opt any-thing, even most spiritual practices, so as to expand it-self"

- JEAN-YVES LELOUP

Bottom line. *We are heading into Pillar Two territory. This chapter is about:*
- *Understanding and applying mindfulness*
- *Creating mindfulness practices*

MINDFULNESS

Mindfulness is a mental state that is achieved by focusing one's awareness on the present moment, while calmly acknowledging and accepting one's feelings, thoughts, and bodily sensations. It is sometimes used as a therapeutic technique.

Rick Hanson, Ph.D. and one of the leading scientific minds on the brain and mindfulness said, "Only we humans worry about the future, regret the past and blame ourselves for the present."

It's tough to create a happy, successful, fulfilling and satisfying life from a place of blame. And we all do it in various ways. It impacts areas of our lives from our happiness, to our focus, and even the health of our physical body.

Mindfulness is a massive topic and we cannot possible cover it all here. There are entire books written just on the subject. If I were to make one suggestion it would be Rick Hanson's <u>Buddha's Brain</u>.

You can create your own mindfulness rituals and practices and here are a few great places to start.

YOU'RE A WINNER

Start counting your wins. We unintentionally and naturally focus on the negative or what's wrong. Because of this default human setting we have to focus more intentionally on the positive. At the end of the day we often spend the time right before bed focusing on what we need to do, didn't do or could have done better. This not only prevents us from getting into an optimal sleep state, but it puts our focus on the negative squarely in our sub-conscious.

Create a daily practice of counting your wins. Wins might be anything from flossing regularly to eating healthy, connecting with your kids, meditating, completing a project or landing that huge business deal. This can be as simple as jotting your wins down before bed in a Win Journal, having a conversation with your partner in which you each share your wins, creating a win jar where you jot down wins on post it notes and throw the notes in the jar to be looked at when you aren't feeling great or need a "pick me up."

BE GRATEFUL

It's free! Gratitude is everything. Start or end your day (or both!) with a gratitude journal. It's been proven to improve your happiness levels by as much as 10%. After a few weeks of this daily practice, the results have been shown to last as long as 7 months, even if the practice is discontinued. This is as simple as writing down 3-5 things you are grateful for and why. You can do this as you wait for the coffee to brew or right before you close your eyes to go to bed.

FIND YOUR CALM

Create a meditation practice. Meditation is proven to support health by reducing anxiety and various physical and stress related diseases. Your daily mediation practice can be anywhere from 3 minutes for a beginner to 20-minute sessions, or even much longer, once or twice a day.

And if you need some social proof, most successful people meditate, including Oprah, Tony Robbins, Russell Simmons, Tom Hanks, Ellen Degeneres, and Tim Ferris. Steve Jobs was also a regular meditator.

If you need a little help, use an app like Headspace or Insight Timer. My favorite teacher, David Ji, has free guided mediations on his website.

YOUR TURN:

1) Take on at least one practice to grow your mindfulness: a win's list, gratitude, or meditation.

2) Notice when you are avoiding being present (thinking about the past or worrying about the future).

3) Spend at least one hour per day with your phone turned off being fully present to another person or in nature.

13 | YOUR KING KONG

◆ ◆ ◆

"Depending on what they are, our habits will either make us or break us. We become what we repeatedly do."

- SEAN COVEY

Bottom line. *Routine, it has the power to make or break your life. This chapter is about:*
- *Understanding the value of a routine*
- *Creating a powerful routine*

ROUTINE
THE KING KONG OF SUCCESS!

I tell people all the time, my life wouldn't have changed, I wouldn't have written this book, gotten healthy, generated more joy, fulfillment and peace of mind without my morning ritual. Now my morning routine isn't the right routine for you. That is for you to create and decide yourself.

Cycles and routine are part of nature. The sun and moon have a cycle and routine. The seasons have a routine. Animals and plants have a routine in their reproduction, seed productions and in their survival. But as humans, we have the power to avoid or create empowered or subconsciously create disempowered routines.

My routine became the heartbeat of my life and it's actually my favorite part of the day. And over time it's evolved and changed.

What does my morning routine look like?

It has gone through different incarnations, but I'll share my basic recipe.

They start at night. Since my ideal morning routine takes place early in the morning, I need to be able to wake up with ample time to support my desired routine. That means I need to be in bed by around 10 or 10:30pm. That usually also means I need to have shut down technology, phone, TV and computer by 9:30pm at the latest.

The reason I need to be in bed by 10 or 10:30pm is I like to read for 30 to 60 minutes to end the day. Remember this is all part of my routine. Reading something light, relaxing, spiritual and yet positive before bed is the way I set myself up for an easy, peaceful and restful night sleep. If I'm not asleep by 11pm, it makes waking up between 4am-6am very challenging.

I want to be clear, this particular routine isn't for everyone. Some people need more than 6 hours of sleep. I function very well on 6 to 7 hours of good sleep, but some people need more like 7 to 8 or even 8 to 9. You need to determine this, but you also need to set yourself up for success. If waking up early is key, then create a bedtime and bedtime routine that will make the early wake up possible. This isn't rocket science, it's commitment, practice, and integrity, meaning doing what you say you will do.

A common example: I want to wake up early, but you think you can't. Anyone can wake up early. Anyone! Don't give me this "I'm not a morning person." You just aren't going to bed early enough, haven't practiced it enough or you aren't committed enough to the results you want that the morning routine is designed to support you with. That's a huge point here. If you want something badly enough, you will do what it takes. So, if you are struggling to wake up in the morning, you either haven't powerfully chosen or you just don't want it or the benefits badly enough. And making changes isn't easy, if it was, we'd all be doing it all the time. So, choosing to create a routine is critical.

If you in fact do, stop making excuses and find a way to do it won't always be peachy. There are some days in which my alarm goes off and I honestly don't want to wake up. But I think about what I want, why I want it and drag myself out of the bed. It's a choice that you also have the opportunity to make regarding your routine if it will support you in making your goals a reality.

Back to my example, after I wake up and get the basics out of the way, teeth brushed and bathroom, I drink a glass of room temp lemon water. As I'm drinking it, I get the coffee pot started. After drinking the water, I sit down and meditate for 20 minutes. After I complete my meditation, I grab my coffee with my favorite creamer; I just love starting the day with something delicious. As I sip my coffee, I grab a journal and do a series of exercises.

I write down 3-5 things I'm grateful for and why.

I write down 3 things that would make today a great day.

I write down a powerful "I AM..." statement/affirmation, such as "I AM UNREASONABLE." I then put this affirmation somewhere I will remember it all day.

I then write down the 3 biggest goals I am currently working on as if they have already happened, such as, "I am a published author and Fictional Authenticity is a best seller. "

Lastly, I write one thing I'm grateful for about money.

Remember, these are my steps. This is not the "right" routine, just my routine.

After this part is complete, I typically read for anywhere from 20 minutes to an hour. I usually have a morning book that is something inspiring and motivating.

After reading, I do something physical, such as Hot Yoga, the gym with weights and some cardio, a few laps in the pool and/or just some push-ups, pull-ups, and sit ups.

And somedays the physical exercise comes first. And other days I might cut out one thing or two. But to establish this powerful routine, I was pretty focused and committed to doing it all daily for about a year.

Over time I have done more adjusting and tweaking, because I have come to better understand who I am and what I need on a daily basis. For instance, when I was living in New

York, I needed more meditation, yoga, and reading. I needed to slow down because the fast-paced rat race was so tense. Living in San Diego, I don't need as much meditation or reading, I do more win counting, gratitude, and other tools to get me in the right mindset to work hard as it's a slower pace.

I'm a big believer that everyone needs to create their own routine that fits the life that they want to create and supports the person they want to be. My routine does that for me, and I have structured it so it can take anywhere from 30 mins to 3 or 4 hours, if we're including the workout. I deeply believe this routine is the most well spent energy and time in my entire day.

I will add, if you aren't clear on your "What For" taking this on is going to be much more challenging. If you have a powerful "What For" it will support you in the challenges that arise in the process.

Tim Ferris, Author of the 4-Hour Work Week, 4-Hour Body, Tools of Titans and the Podcast "The Tim Ferris Show", has asked hundreds of successful people about their morning rituals and has created a list of 5 that he incorporates into his life: Making his Bed, Meditating for 10-20 minutes, at least 30 seconds of light exercise, drinking strong tea, and writing in a journal for 5-10 minutes.

"And if you win the morning, you win the day."

- TIM FERRIS

We all know Tony Robbins. He's the world's most successful performance coach and he's also a billionaire. He's coached people like President Bill Clinton, Nelson Mandela, Serena Williams and other people at the highest levels of success.

Robbins' routine has also changed over the years, but he ensures he gets at least 10-15 minutes every day for his routine regardless of what is going on. Robbins' routine consists of a cold plunge or cryotherapy tanks to shock his system, breathing exercises, expressing gratitude, prayer and then eating in a way in which food is fuel, not pleasure.

So, whether you want to create a morning routine that takes 10 minutes every morning or something that takes a few hours, let's create it here.

How did I create my routine, you might be asking?

There is no right way. As long as you haven't been living under a rock, I'm sure you have heard of, or already know a bunch of practices you can incorporate. It's pretty likely you've heard of meditation, yoga, reading, the gym, the sauna, breathing exercises, prayer, a gratitude journal, bedtime or wake up time, and affirmations. Again, these may not be the right things for you, but these are a few options. Another place to look is your well-being list. Are there things on that list that if you did them every day you know you would see improvement in your life, your productivity, your joy, your satisfaction, your energy levels, relationships and your health?

When I originally created my list, I was already reading and meditating daily. But I wasn't practicing any gratitude, so I added that into my morning routine. At that point I wasn't reading in the mornings and I recognized the benefits of reading something that lifts me up, inspires me and sets the tone for the day, so I also incorporated that into my routine. Lots of the things I incorporated into my routine came right off my well-being list. They were things I wanted to be doing every day.

Now what about you?

How much time do you want to incorporate into your routine and when will you incorporate it into your day? I highly encourage a morning routine, but you need to choose for you. Simply choose and commit to this.

So how long? Is it 10 minutes, 30, an hour or more? And when? Will this be Monday-Friday or seven days a week?

Right now, let's not worry about how we are going to make this happen or how we will work it into our lives, let's just create the routine that we know will empower us to start living the lives we are committed to.

We will talk about this more later, but that "How" that you are thinking about is the biggest killer of dreams, goals, and ideas, and frankly it's not relevant. Why and What are all that matter. How is just a road block. So, for now, try and ignore it.

What do you want your morning routine to consist of?

Here are some more ideas: A run or walk, making your bed, setting a daily intention, uninterrupted play time with your child, a green smoothie, creative writing, reading the newspaper, walking on the beach, playing with a pet, dancing, singing, watching funny videos, and exercise. There are many more, you can even invent things of your own. Maybe a motorcycle ride down a long highway works for you. Or morning sex. Or maybe it's telling everyone you live with why you love them. It doesn't matter, except that it's a routine, which means you do it daily or on days you choose, and it supports the life and person you are committed to being.

YOUR TURN:

1) Create an AM Routine

2) Create a PM Routine

3) Practice sticking to your routines for 30 days, notice what shifts.

14 | DON'T GET CAUGHT LEAKING... INTEGRITY

◆ ◆ ◆

"With integrity, you have nothing to fear, since you have nothing to hide. With integrity, you will do the right thing, so you will have no guilt."

- ZIG ZIGLAR

Bottom line. *This chapter is going to move you forward and this is how:*
- *Understanding integrity*
- *Creating a powerful relationship to your integrity*

IT'S PERSONAL

"Integrity is the essence of everything successful."

- R. BUCKMINSTER FULLER

For me, integrity means "being" your word, living by what you said long after the feelings of wanting to do what you said have faded. You will wake up and not "feel" like making the bed, eating healthy, working out, writing that book, making 100 more sales calls, trying to get a building permit or even having that hard conversation with your partner. To create the lives we desire, we have to go beyond what we want, comfort, and being committed, and how can you be committed without integrity.

Integrity isn't a moral conversation, it's a personal one. You are the only one who determines your integrity. It is also not a black and white conversation. You can have integrity when it comes to others, yet not have much when it comes to yourself. You can have integrity around one project and be out of integrity when it comes to another.

The unmistakable aspect of integrity however is nothing great happens without it. I believe integrity to be at the pinnacle with well-being; if you don't take care of yourself you can't do or be anything. And if you don't have integrity you won't be, do or fulfill on your commitments and desires.

WHAT STOPS US

Most of us don't have an issue saying what we want to do, be, have, or create. Yet, many more of us have trouble completing or fulfilling what we said we wanted to do or become.

What stops us?

Well it's different for everyone, but things range from "no plan, no commitment, no direction, didn't feel like it," to "I didn't really want to, I wasn't motivated, or I had no time." But my absolute favorite is other things came up. It's my favorite because of course things came up. That's life. That's what happens. If things didn't come up, life would be pretty uneventful. And those things that just came up, well, they're just called circumstances.

What separates those who achieve greatness and success and those who don't, is choosing to have unrelenting integrity when it comes to their commitments. Being a person who moves forward in respect to their commitments, regardless of how they feel or what circumstances and obstacles stand in their way accomplish their goals.

Let's look at integrity through the lens of driving somewhere and getting a flat tire. The differences between someone who just decides to change their plans because they got a flat tire, and someone who is determined to get where they are going regardless of the flat tire is monumental. One is a person who MIGHT do what they say they are going to do. The other is a person who DOES what they said they are going to do. Integrity is simply the result of choosing to fulfill on their declaration no matter what circumstances arise.

Think about a map, there are all sorts of ways to get to the same place. In the theoretical map we don't have any idea which way will be the most successful. We know which direction might get us there fastest if nothing gets in the way, but in life rarely does nothing get in the way. This is where integrity comes in. If you don't have it, when circumstances arise you are going to use those as excuses and reasons to debunk your commitments.

It's easy, we do it all the time. Think about the last few things you said you wanted, or take it a step further, what are you committed to? I ask that because wants can change, but commitments are stickier. So, let's go ahead and make a list of all the reasons why you don't have the things you want. Why don't you have the job, the money, the partner, the success? Why haven't you written the book, gotten the promotion? Why don't you have the new car, the fancy watch? Why aren't you just happy?

Write down all the reasons you don't have what you want.

After you've completed that list, look at it. What's on the list? Is it a list of to-do's? A list of wants? Commitments? Actions?

Likely, it's not. Likely, it's a list of circumstances and excuses. And while I am totally empathetic for deeply emotional circumstances like deaths, break-ups and serious well-being issues, they are still circumstances.

People die.

People get sick.

People lose their jobs.

People get divorces and break up.

This is life and while we can love each other, get supported and take time to be with loss and feelings, we can't let what life throw at us stop us from living it to the fullest.

...Well, we can. But likely when it's the end of your days you'll be regretting that you let one circumstance, excuse, and reason after another stop you.

Imagine what life would be like if you consistently kept your commitments and kept your word. If you did what you said you would do, with others, with yourself, with your projects, at your job, with friends and family. Imagine if no matter what life threw at you, you kept going. You kept moving forward and you were able to be and do and live the life you really wanted.

Now there are some of you out there thinking "well you don't understand (fill in your situation)."

It might be that your partner left you as a single parent, or maybe they just work a lot, so you feel as though you are a single parent. Maybe you have a boss that is impossible to please, so it doesn't seem to matter what you say you will do because they are always changing their mind. Maybe you feel like you can't stick to anything because your job or kids are always springing things on you.

I'm sorry, if you are having a hard time. Life isn't always fair or kind, and unfortunately neither are other people. And if you want to change your life or create the life of your dreams the circumstances don't matter, they are all just excuses. And most of us stop here, where it gets challenging or difficult, and the circumstances won't let us.

Most of us don't keep going and generate the results we committed to regardless of what comes up. And if by chance you think your circumstances are 110% unique to you, do me a quick favor and look online for someone who's done something great, amazing or life changing with circumstances like yours. They exist. The difference between them and you, they didn't let their circumstances stop them!

"The supreme quality for leadership is unquestionably integrity. Without it, no real success is possible, no matter whether it is on a section gang, a football field, in an army or in an office."

- DWIGHT D. EISENHOWER

YOUR TURN:

1) What are some small steps that you could take to improve your relationship to integrity? Is it getting to meetings on time? Waking up when you said you would? Create 1-3 small goals like these and complete them.

2) What are the commitments you have that you are not fulfilling on? Notice what they are. Create one structure that will support you in fulfilling on them starting today. For example, if you have a commitment to your well-being, go schedule a nonnegotiable hour in your calendar where you get to go work out. (If you are stuck, the next chapter will help you)

3) Practice being your word. Notice where you are able to, and where it becomes more challenging. Notice what circumstances make it acceptable for your to not be your word.

4) Practice sticking to things you decided to do, even if you no longer feel like it. What does it take for you to do it even if you "don't feel like it?"

15 | WANT TO WIN?

◆ ◆ ◆

"Competing at the highest level is not about winning. It's about preparation, courage, understanding and nurturing your people, and heart. Winning is the result."

- JOE TORRE

Bottom line. *Here is the final piece of the pillar puzzle. This chapter is about:*
- *Creating structures that are empowering and will have you win*
- *Creating structures sufficient to the levels of resistance we are dealing with*
- *Understanding the value of affirmations*
- *Learning the power in telling everyone*

STRUCTURES OF SUCCESS

T he last component to this pillar of change is structure. Specifically, the structures you will create or put in place to ensure you actually fulfill on your commitments. We all know how easy it is to say we are going to change behaviors or break habits. We've all said, "no more French fries" or "tomorrow, I will start going to the gym," and we all know sometimes we do and sometimes we don't.

Consider that anything you take on in life that isn't in your comfort zone, that stretches or asks you to behave differently, break patterns or start new ones is going to be challenging. Our natural states, The Hater, The Wimp, and The Cheerleader want us to stay much the same, they are comfortable there. To take on a morning routine or any new practice is going to test you, and to support you in doing what you said we want to create structures that will be sufficient to the resistance that naturally shows up.

For instance, it's Monday, January 5th and the 6am alarm clock goes off. Your New Year's Resolution was to lose those pesky 20 pounds you've been carrying around like a dead body and get back in shape. And this time you are finally going to do it! But what often happens? You're tired, you don't want to wake up, that voice in your head says go back to sleep, you need more sleep, you'll just start tomorrow.

But you won't start tomorrow...likely you play this game all the time.

Or maybe you've made a commitment to making that documentary you've been thinking about but each time you go to start, "things" come up that pull you away.

We all have "things" like this happen. We all become victims of circumstance. What separates people who achieve, create, and are successful is they don't let their circumstances stop them. They set up structures to empower them even when circumstances or situations arise to thwart them.

I had a client who repeatedly made commitments about what she was going to do, how she was going to do it and how it would change her life. She would show up week after week disempowered not having done what she said. We could create accountabilities after accountabilities, but it wasn't having an impact.

One day I proposed a new structure. If she didn't do what she said she was going to do by our next session, she would have to throw $100 out of her car window. She didn't like this idea at all. She also knew what she wanted was the thing she wasn't doing. She saw the value and was scared. She also knew that if she didn't do it, it was going to go up to $200 and double each week there after until we hit a number that was powerful enough that she simply could not do it anymore.

Guess what happened, she did it. She wasn't willing to throw the money out the window and that was strong enough to stand up to her resistance.

Now a structure doesn't have to be money. It can be 5 alarms all over the place to get you out of bed. It can be a text message or phone call from a friend reminding you what you said you were going to do. It can be a series of calendar alarms popping up on your phone and computer reminding you. You can write a series of Post-It notes and post them all over your house, office, in your car, and on your computer screen so you have physical reminders everywhere you look.

It can be signing up for a book club or writing group or

something where you can be held accountable. It can be creating rewards that you get when you do what you said. For instance, one straight week of completing your morning ritual equals a trip to the spa or a beach day with friends. Maybe one month of straight morning rituals get you the reward of a three days weekend.

Regardless, rewards or consequences, setting up a structure to support you in generating results is the key.

So what's it going to be?

How will you ensure that you powerfully fulfill on your new morning routine or any of your new commitments?

Consider and answer the following questions:

How will you remember to do it?

Can you couple it with anything else? (Coupling is when you tie two things together. For example, I already brush my teeth every day, now I'm going to meditate immediately after I brush my teeth.)

What will you do when time or circumstances seem to get in the way?

What plans do you need to make (like waking up earlier) to create the ideal situation so you can fulfill your declaration?

What support do you need (alarms, reminders, accountability buddies)?

Do you need a reward to motivate you? What will it be?

Do you need a consequence to hold you accountable? What will it be?

Perfect, when will you start?

Before we wrap up this chapter, let's look at a few other

structures for success.

AFFIRMATIONS

I think by now many of us know and are familiar with the concept of an affirmation. But for those of us new to personal development, thanks for being here! It's hard work, you deserve it.

An affirmation is a positive personal statement or declaration written in the first person aimed at altering the conscious and subconscious mind.

> *"An affirmation opens the door. It's a beginning point on a path to change. In essence, you're saying to your subconscious mind: I am taking responsibility. I am aware that there is something I can do to change.'*

> - LOUISE HAY

I am a big believer in affirmations, and while I stand by them and believe them to be effective, simply saying "I am a brilliant inventor who makes millions of dollars from my life changing inventions" doesn't actually do or create anything.

However, while it alone might not change anything, doing anything different with thoughts or actions can change everything. So, altering the way you think of yourself could have you get off the couch and start inventing.

The book, <u>The Secret,</u> focused mostly on positive thoughts, beliefs, and things like Affirmations. But, for me what is missing is the cleaning up of the old thought patterns and creating new actions and patterns.

We can't simply wish we were rich and have a great body

while sitting on the couch eating burritos and waiting for something to happen. That's not a thing!

We can start by thinking it and believing it and then generating action. Together anything becomes possible.

There are three parts to a powerful process of changing the way you think and adding affirmations into your life.

First, you must start noticing the thoughts that are showing up. The voice that you hear in your head saying, "I suck," or "I'm not good enough," or whatever. The first step is identifying these limiting beliefs and negative self-talk. Catch yourself saying it to yourself. Simply notice and hear the voice. Pause and be mindful.

That alone, noticing it, and pausing to generate awareness around it is a massive shift. Then you can say "while it feels real, it's not actually true." As you begin to clean up the mess that your mind creates you can start to craft new messages to tell yourself, affirmations.

Let's create some affirmations that would support you in living the life you want to create.

The brilliant, leader, author, doctor, and organization expert Dr. Stephen R. Covey says it best in his book, <u>The 7 Habits of Highly Effective People</u>.

> "A good affirmation has five basic ingredients, it's personal, it's positive, it's present tense, it's visual, and it's emotional. So I might write something like this, 'It is deeply satisfying (emotional) that I (personal) respond (present tense) with wisdom, love, firmness, and self-control (positive) when my children misbehave."
>
> - DR. STEPHEN R. COVEY

One of my favorite affirmations is very simple, "I am strong, healthy in body and mind and I love myself exactly the way I am."

Another is even simpler, "I am love, I am loved, I am whole and complete. I am loving awareness."

Let's create a few affirmations now that you can incorporate into your own life. I encourage you to read, write, or even record and listen to them daily. Sometimes something as little as 10 times in the AM or PM can have a powerful impact. And I get it. If you are new to this or have tried this before, you might be skeptical and that's okay.

Consider you are fighting an uphill battle as your Hater, Wimp and Cheerleader are constantly affirming things daily over and over again. Think about it, we are unconsciously saying what are really negative affirmations all day long.

"I'm fat."

"I'm ugly."

"I'm not smart enough."

We are now simply training our brains to use its power in a way that is supportive.

Depending on who you are, and everyone is different, you might want to create an affirmation for your health, your body, your mind, your relationships and your wealth. Anything else works also, but these are great places to start.

Now go!

Have you written some affirmations down? Try spending a full minute with each one twice, daily. Really be with it, visualize and feel it in your body. If you just say it but don't honor it, don't feel it, don't practice believing it, then the power is lost. Mean it, even before it becomes your reality.

Louise Hay is a master at Affirmations and her book, <u>Heal Your Body</u>, is a great resource that I highly recommend.

TELL EVERYONE!

Another great practice is to tell everyone what you are up to.

Seriously, tell them about the book you are writing, the diet you are on, the trainer you are hiring, the coach or program you just signed up for. Tell everyone what you are up to, and why you are up to it.

Think about this.

When we keep things to ourselves, it's easy to just quit. Nobody knows, we don't have to be with anyone else's thoughts or options, we just get to know we didn't do another thing. But if we tell the world we are writing a book or tell the world we are going to lose weight, it's easy to get supported but also harder to quit as we have declared it publicly.

Get out there and tell everyone what you are up to! Tell them what you are doing, building, creation and dreaming about!

Do it now!

Write down the names of 10 people with whom will share your goals.

Now, go share them!

A REMINDER

There are a million structures to support yourself in growing, changing, being committed and accomplishing your goals. But there is no right way. What works for someone might not work at all for someone else. But at the end of the day no structure can make you do anything.

The alarm doesn't make me get to 6am yoga, I make me. The alarm just beeps because I set it to beep. Plenty of people reading this book, and out there in the world, know they turn that baby off as soon as it beeps, or they get into a conversation in their head debating if they should get up for that workout or if they need more sleep. For many of us the commitment doesn't win.

While we can come up with tons of accountabilities and structures to support us, the only thing that can have anything in our lives change is us! That's it. You! You are making a choice and making a commitment and doing it because you said so. Because you know how important it is for you.

And every time it comes time to do the things you have committed to and those voices in your head start yapping or circumstances arise that seem to get in your way, you can practice simply pausing, hearing all the noise and *choosing* to dismiss it and proceed as planned with your commitment.

Nobody said growth or change was easy. It's a process, but that doesn't mean it has to be hard. Easy and hard are relative, they aren't factual. Your change, your growth, your improvement and your transformation can be whatever you want it to be, it's your choice.

Choose powerfully and wisely in service of the commitments you have made. Because that's all a great life is, one choice after another in service of what you said you wanted.

YOUR TURN:

1) If you have not already, choose at least one mindfulness practice that you are willing to integrate into your life. Put it into your schedule and start practicing.

2) Come up with 3-5 affirmations and practice them daily. Refer to page 90 for some examples.

3) Create 3-5 structures for your success.

16 | THE BLUEPRINT

◆ ◆ ◆

"If you don't know where you are going, you'll end up someplace else."

Bottom Line: *Your fear and unwillingness are your own worst enemies and in the way of your goals. This chapter is about:*
- *Creating a clear and measurable plan*
- *Distinguishing what will get in the way even with the best plan*
- *Understanding how surrender and vulnerability make goals possible*
- *Dismantling Perfection*

THE BIG PLAN

This Yogi Berra quote is an example of one of the biggest problems I see and hear with people I know, work with, and experience out in the world.

Think about the last time you ordered an Uber or a Lyft. Think about the process.

You open the app, it likely identifies where you are, or you tell it where you are.

Then it asks, "where are you going?"

Have you ever tried to type in "somewhere cool" or "A Place I'll Like?"

Well if you try, you will discover nothing will happen. It won't error, it won't move you forward, and it won't correct you, it will just provide no results and wait until you answer its question, "where are you going?"

Now when you type in an address or give it the name of an exact location, it locates a car, finds multiple routes, and even gives you an estimated time of arrival and price.

Answering Uber's question, my friends, is the perfect example of how to get where you want to go. Most of us, however, aren't actually willing to say with clarity, focus, precision and commitment "where we are going." And because we aren't willing to take that tiny but massive step, the "screen" produces no results and we don't get anywhere.

So far, we've talked about the importance of a solid foundation and taking care of yourself. But even when you have those things handled, the next big obstacle between you and any of your aspirations is your unwillingness to create and declare an actual goal.

#GOALS

I want to be clear what I mean when I use the word goal. These four things are the specifics necessary to have an actual goal:

1) It must be clearly defined. An address is clearly defined. An impartial person can determine if you have arrived at your destination if the address matches your request.
2) It must be measurable. An amount of money, a time limit, a weight, or a frequency are all measurable. A measure assures that even a third party could agree the goal has been achieved.
3) It must be in the future and something you can move towards. While that seems obvious, it's an important component.
4) You must know the *Why* behind what you want to get, achieve, or create.

IT'S OBVIOUS, BUT...

You might be reading this and thinking, this is so obvious, how could someone not know this? And yet, whenever I meet a new person--whether it's through networking, friendship, or the possibility of working together--often I ask them what their goals are and guess what? They are vague, not measurable, often exist without any time frame. And, very often, the person can't articulate why they want this goal.

The key to understanding and setting goals is looking through the lens of an impartial audience. Would the impartial person know, understand, and be able to determine with no opinion whether the goal was achieved or not?

So why don't we do this with our goals or our lives? Why do so many of us, over and over again, create what we think are goals but clearly are just obscure desires and wishes?

Because we are scared.

What if we actually did commit and decided to go for the things we wanted? What if we planned, told others, organized, researched, trained and headed on our way...and then we didn't get there?

What if we simply failed or it was more difficult than expected?

What if we changed our minds or we really didn't want what we thought we wanted?

What then?

I believe most of us are afraid. Not afraid of actual things, but afraid of the things our mind tells us to fear. The things that people might think about us. The things our fear stories taught us. That we aren't good enough. That we will fail or disappoint people. That we won't be accepted. Aren't smart enough or pretty enough.

This fear is why we shy away from creating really big powerful inspiring goals!

I don't believe it's because we don't know how.

I believe it's because we are afraid to shine brightly.

To be seen.

To be heard.

To fail.

To dream and have our hearts broken.

If you deeply and truly want something, it requires you lay

your heart out there on the line. It requires you to be with the possibility that you won't get it. That it won't happen. But it also means you agree to be with the possibility that it will happen. That you won't stop until you get it. That you will create it and you can make your wildest dreams come true.

Since childhood most of us have been heartbroken by something, someone or ourselves. We've been let down. Broken. Disappointed. We've had dreams and seen them evaporate or been told that we can't achieve them, they aren't realistic, or that they are impossible.

We've forgotten how to dream. But even more important we've forgot how to chase the dreams we still have.

And I'm not sure we want to remember because remembering might be heartbreaking. That pain is visceral, something we can still feel and aren't sure we want to feel again.

Dreaming and building dreams takes courage. It takes a brave person to put their heart and ego on the line. Most people won't do it. Most people will live their lives playing it safe. Keeping their hearts, dreams, and deepest desires close to the vest. They won't take a risk or a chance. They recoil at the first challenge or fear that strikes them.

Being here, reading this book, taking on these practices is a step in the right direction.

Just reading these words is a sign that you are open and brave enough to be vulnerable and might just be willing and vulnerable enough to go for what you want.

Are you ready to dream?

Are you brave enough to deal with the heartbreak, the circumstances, the obstacles and the roadblocks that lay ahead?

Are you ready to create that dream?

Are you willing to build a plan that can get you where you want to go?

If you answered yes, yes, yes, or maybe Hell Yes! Let's do this!

GOOGLE MAP YOUR LIFE

Let's start by creating the Blueprint.

What if you could just Google Map your life?

Think about how when you want to get somewhere, you just type it into Google Maps. The app then does the work to figure out all the different routes, to consider traffic, to consider the mode of transportation. While it gives you options, ultimately each set of directions will get you to where you want to go.

Think about building a home. We don't just look at the architect and say, "do your thing."

We sit down with an architect and we discuss what we want, what the finished product will be. The architect creates a Blueprint, a plan to get us from where we are to where we want to be. What I love about housebuilding as an example is that there will still be surprises. Something wasn't level the first time it was measured. Having a bathtub in every bathroom seemed like a good idea until the cost of copper piping went up. But even with the unexpected circumstances, you know where you are headed and can make decisions accordingly from your commitments not feelings.

You have the Blueprint that will support you in heading in the direction of your ultimate intended outcome, regardless of what shows up along the way.

"Unless commitment is made, there are only promises and hopes; but no plans."

- PETER DRUCKER

Do you get why stating your goal and then creating a plan that is based on clear and measurable goals is key? Do you understand why knowing why you want this thing in the future is so important?

Let's look at a way to create your personal blueprint. I call it The DreamMason's Blueprint. It's a map, or a Blueprint, to get you from where you are, to where you want to be.

Now, I always suggest you work with a Coach when using something like this. A Coach can call you out, notice where you're cutting corners. A Coach will see when you are lying to yourself, or simply might need accountability. It's like having a Co-Pilot; it's not their job to fly the plane but to support you, have your back while you're doing it and notice things you might have not seen or missed.

"A goal without a plan is just a wish."

- ANTOINE DE SAINT-EXUPERY

THE DREAMMASON'S BLUEPRINT

Below is a step by step exercise for creating and laying out your goal and generating a clear plan towards it.

Step 1: The Proprietary Goal

This is your Final Destination. Be specific! Vague goals will reap even vaguer results and outcomes. When I say specific, I meant that if a random person was watching they would be able to see that you got where you said you wanted to go. This means there was a measure that wasn't simply an opinion. Also, consider that there is a time by when you will achieve this goal. And again, when I say time, be specific, not summer of 2022, that's a slippery slope. July 8, 2021 is clear.

Step 2: The Anchor

Your Anchor is your *Why*! If you are challenged in figuring out why, I strongly recommend you read Simon Sinek's NY Times Best Seller, <u>Start With Why</u>. Why are you even doing this? Why does it matter? Why? Get very clear on this. If you don't have a powerful reason for going after something, likely when times get tough, when you hit a bump in the road, and you want to quit you will. If you have a powerful Anchor, it can keep you firmly planted in your commitment when even the roughest circumstances arise.

Do not go on to Step 3 if you haven't powerfully created your Anchor!!!

Step 3: The Design

This is often the most fun part. It's like getting to really imagine what the house of your dreams looks like when it's complete. Close your eyes. Imagine the future after The Proprietary Goal is reached. What will be different about your life, about the life of your family and friends? What will be different about how you live or what you do every day? How will you look and feel? Imagine all the ways life will be different. After you have a clear picture of this in your mind, write it out or even draw a picture of it, if you're an artist of course. I love the idea of you using your artistic and creative abilities to draw out what your future looks like, that's powerful. What I like to do, because I cannot draw is write a letter to myself.

Dear Alex... and describe in as much detail, feelings, and emotions as possible what the future looks like from the future.

This is very similar to the Back to the Future exercise, which we have already discussed, but around a specific goal.

Step 4: Your Tool Box

What's in your tool box? You have tons of skills, talents, abilities, and knowledge already. It would be silly to go to Home Depot to buy tools to build your house without taking a look to see what tools you already have. What do you already have that is going to support you in making this Proprietary Goal or dream into a reality? Write out the Talents, Abilities, Skills, and Knowledge you already have. Don't let yourself off the hook without identifying at least 5 to 10.

Step 5: Quantity Survey

And just like above, if you know you've never owned a hammer, you'd probably have that on the list of things you need from Home Depot. The Quantity Survey is an opportunity to look at what you already know you'll likely need when it comes to skills, abilities or knowledge, or expertise. This doesn't mean that you will have to learn them or that you will have to hire someone. It's simply taking into account what you know you don't know.

Step 6: The Grout

Grout fills in gaps. There will be gaps. So what tools, resources or people do you know of that can support you in filling in the gaps? For instance, if your friend Bob is a Plumber and you know you will eventually need a Plumber, then Bob is clearly a resource and you would identify him here as Plumbing support. Now create an in-depth and specific list. Be specific, this will help you later when you notice there are gaps and you need support.

If you know you need something that you don't have resource-wise, like you know you will need an electrician but you don't know any, this is a great place to make note of that also.

Step 7: Treat Yourself

This is often my clients' favorite part. It's time to create some treats, ways to reward yourself for all your hard work. The idea here is to take the time to acknowledge yourself for following your plan. This shit can be scary! And you are doing it. Create several different treats that might signify different types of wins or successes along the way. Brainstorm a bunch, the more the better.

And don't forget to create the Grand Prize for completing the Proprietary Goal!

Step 8: Reinforcement

Now what happens when the plan, the steps, the commitments and the treats aren't enough to get you to do what you said you would do? What happens when you say over and over you'll start today or tomorrow or you'll do that thing and you don't? The reinforcement comes into play! That's what happens. Come up with 1-3 consequences that don't hurt or impact/sabotage other goals. For instance, "If I don't make the 10 calls to get clients then I can't go to the gym," that might be sabotaging well-being. But saying, "If I don't make the 10 calls I can't watch my favorite TV shows until I make the calls," likely isn't sabotaging anything.

Reinforcements can be mild consequences like taking things away, or steep consequences like throwing hard earned Benjamins out the window of your car while driving if you don't do the thing you said you would do.

Step 9: The Specifications

These are the specific checkpoints along the way. During a marathon there are markers that support runners, so they know how far they have come and how far they have to go. Often with larger projects we think about simply getting to the next checkpoint. With Specifications I'm asking you to create these in advance so as you embark on your journey you always know you are on the right path. Look at your Proprietary Goal and create Specifications with dates in which they will be reached that you want to hit along the way that will ensure you are going in the right direction. There is no right or wrong amount but be careful not to put them too close together or too far apart which could be self-sabotage. This is a great place to have a coach look at what you've created.

Step 10: The Millwork

The Millwork is all about the details. What details or things do you need to do, create or make happen to get you to your first Specification? Create as many as you think you need to get to Specification 1 (after you have reached or completed the first specification return to this step and create The Millwork to get your to Specification 2 and repeat until you have worked your way to the end of your Proprietary Goal). Example: I have a goal of buying my first home. The first specification is to save $10,000 over the next 3 months. While that's not nearly enough to buy a home, it's the first Specification that when I hit it, I would know I'm on my way.

The Millwork might be setting up a Mint account to monitor all my money and ensure I know where every dollar is going and what is being saved. Another aspect of the millwork might be to save $25 a day, by not buying coffees or lunches out. Another aspect of millwork might be to make 10% more sales over the next month to increase my income.

Step 11: Specification Treats

Let's look back at Step 7, where you created treats. Now let's take those treats and combine them to the Specifications or even really challenging pieces of Millwork. When you accomplish The Specification or that challenging aspect of Millwork you get to treat yourself with a treat. I often assign Reinforcements to a few of the Specifications or The Millwork also, and if I don't do, be or accomplish said task or action the Reinforcement kicks in.

Step 12 (Bonus Step): Support Structures

This is one of the most powerful steps and it's a bonus because we don't always need it, but likely if we think we don't, we do. So besides Treats and Reinforcements what people, and or reminders, could you put in place to support you in doing what you said you would do? This could apply to the Specifications or to the Millwork. A great support structure might be letting others know what your goals are so you can be accountable. Another might be creating an accountability buddy that supports you.

REAL TALK

Generating The DreamMason's Blueprint will not guarantee or ensure you accomplish your goals. Creating it and never looking at it again won't support you much at all. Taking on this exercise, creating it fully, using it, flushing it out, keeping it alive and in your daily routine is essential, and will support you in getting from where you are to where you want to be.

I suggest my clients go through it every Monday to support them in getting focused for the week and determining what they need to be doing, being or creating to generate their goals and dreams.

A Blueprint can only be effective if you use it!

BUT WHAT ABOUT...
AHH CIRCUMSTANCES!

"He is happy whom circumstances suit his temper; but he is more excellent who suits his temper to any circumstance."

- DAVID HUME

We know shit happens. It just does. Literally and figuratively.

Bad things happen. People die. People don't do what they say they are going to do. We make mistakes, fuck up, we drop the ball, we sleep in, hurt others, and betray people we love. The environment and politics around us fall into our laps, accidents happen, and the world keeps spinning.

Regardless of who you are, what you do, how much you plan, prepare and stay positive, life happens and often it doesn't happen according to our plan, what is fair, how we think it should go or was supposed to go. But people who reach their goals, create their dreams and produce and achieve things, do so despite the circumstances that arise.

Circumstances will happen. However, circumstances themselves don't mean much, what matters is who we are in the face of them.

Clients often present amazing excuses, reasons, and stories in relation to their circumstances to justify their situations. And I get it. Shit happens and it's okay. We do get to feel our feelings and be with what happens, but if we let the circumstances and excuses stop us, we won't get where we want to go. It's weird to know that circumstances exist and are normal, and then still use them as an excuse. That doesn't make any sense and it's just our way of letting ourselves off the hook.

Imagine you are in a car and are headed to the hot new restaurant in town. You are really excited to go, you have been invited along with a ton of your favorite celebrities, heroes, idols, mentors, people you admire and even family and friends. You feel so fortunate and lucky to have been invited. Consider feeling so excited that you know no matter what happens you will get there.

When suddenly, you hit traffic. Bumper to bumper traffic. Do you turn around and quit? Likely you find another way to get there or just be with the traffic until it passes.

Now what if you got two flat tires? You only have one spare and you can't quickly change it. Some people might give up. Some people might get discouraged. But this is the biggest night of your life filled with every single person that inspires you! You could walk, find a bike, call a rideshare, call a friend, or even hitchhike. If you are committed to accomplishing something, nothing, besides death, can stop you.

When we are totally committed to what we want and where we are going, we are willing to create anything despite our circumstances. We only fail when we choose to quit or give in to our circumstances and let them control our success or control the outcome.

Choose to keep going, keep shifting, keep adjusting, and you will get to where you are headed.

IT'S PREDICTABLE

"Nothing splendid has ever been achieved except by those who dared believe that something inside them was superior to circumstance."

- BRUCE BARTON

Now if you know and will admit that circumstances mess with our plans, let's create a list of predictable circumstances that will likely get in your way of the Blueprint you just created.

For instance:
- I don't have enough money.
- A client could fire me.
- Parent, Family or Partner is not supportive.
- There is not enough time.
- Grandma gets sick and I have to take care of her.
- I have kids that are starting school.
- I have to move.
- Had an emergency
- I lost my job
- Got mugged
- Going on Vacation
- etc.

Go ahead and list yours.

Now let's decide what you will do when the predicable things happen.

Decide how you will stay the course and write those down, so when they happen you can refer to this list.

Remember life is circumstance. Things happen. Life doesn't go as planned. It isn't fair, nobody said it would be. Nobody created how it should go or is supposed to go, it just goes. Often it's not what we want or would have chosen, and you need to keep going to create the life you want in spite of what happens.

SURRENDER

This all sounds great, right? You have a goal. You just got a way to map out your goal. You are getting ahead of circumstances and planning so they don't sink your ship.

And now, I must ask you to release one more circumstance. Are you willing to simply play the game without it needing to go perfectly according to plan? This, my friends, is the circumstance that often messes with everyone's head.

In Brene Brown's book, Daring Greatly, she writes about how joy inherently leaves us vulnerable to disappointment, and because of that we sabotage our ability to experience joy. I believe this works equally with love.

I bring this in now because we have become so accustomed to expecting the worst, and wanting to avoid heartbreak that we use things, like circumstances, to protect ourselves. We think they protect us from hurt but they also protect us from caring a lot, falling in love, chasing our dreams or being able to feel our real feelings. We have become a world of those waiting for "the other shoe to drop" dampening our light, lessoning our power and muting our ability to live authentically.

So, what do we do about it?

We accept that circumstances happen, and we decide who we will be when they happen.

We surrender. We give up the notion or the belief that we can control anything and everything. We can't. It's not possible. That vice grip you have on your life, your relationships, your job, your perfection, your desire to look strong, cool, confident, pretty, or anything else is preventing you from being you, expressing yourself and living as the person you truly are.

What does it mean to surrender? The dictionary defines surrender as, "to yield or to give up." When I first heard that I needed to surrender, I thought that's bullshit, I'm not giving up. I'm not going to just give in.

My coach shared his definition of surrender, which is, "to put down your defenses. To stop fighting against and allow."

I took some time personally to really process what my coach had shared with me. The more I thought about it, the more it made sense. I was spending a ton of time keeping myself safe as a form of control. I was controlling how I looked, how I came off, who I let myself have feelings for, what I cared about or loved, who I would let in, when I would be honest, vulnerable and authentic. I was spending the majority of my time being hyper vigilant to protect myself from being hurt, disappointed, upset, let down, looking badly or letting others down.

Letting down the control and surrounding requires something else...Vulnerability!

VULNERABILITY

To be vulnerable, we must first surrender our needs to be safe, in control, in power, closed off, and the managers of our lives.

But surrender is tough when we feel we need to be on guard or protected because we spend so much time afraid. Most of us don't want to walk around feeling vulnerable, that would be uncomfortable. But vulnerability is human. Vulnerability is required to live an authentic life. If we aren't being authentic, we are pretending, and if we are pretending, we are hiding or managing who we actually are, which isn't being vulnerable. Your Fictionally Authentic life was in many ways built on the backbone of an unwillingness to be vulnerable.

We need to talk about vulnerability because circumstances are happening all around us all the time and if we are spending extraordinary amounts of energy trying to avoid them or control them, we aren't allowing ourselves to be ourselves.

We are trying to control our environments, others and ourselves. This leaves little room for us to be authentic. If we aren't authentic, then how can we create the lives we actually want? We will be creating lives we think we can get, or lives we think we should be living or lives we want for reasons outside of ourselves.

Think about how it feels to control something.

Picture this, you have an elephant on a leash, your job is to control it and keep it still. Another person's job is to scare it, make it move and walk. It's going to take a lot of your strength and energy to hold on to that elephant. And no matter what you do with your two arms and how strong you are that elephant isn't going to allow you to be in control.

Consider you are you, the leash is all the areas of your life you are trying to control, manage, manipulate, dominate, and unwilling to surrender to, and that elephant is life and life isn't something that we can control. Life brings it every single day. It brings death, it brings life, it brings hurricanes, earthquakes, rain, snow, traffic accidents, sickness, loss, growth, and all the other surprises we encounter in any given moment.

The energy it requires to control life and others leaves us feeling exhausted, defeated, frustrated, and joyless.

We get to think we are in control and not vulnerable, but the cost is joy and always feeling disappointed.

This creates a watered down, diluted life. We start to expect bad things to happen just so we can plan ways to stop or avoid them. We expect others to let us down, fuck up, break things, cheat, and mostly that things won't go our way. This pushes us to try to control more and more. It becomes a cycle.

No wonder nobody wants to just surrender. If we surrender, imagine the shit storm that would hit. We are trying so hard to hold it all together that the idea of letting go and not pushing against aka surrendering sounds like the worst idea ever.

It's important to remember that surrendering doesn't mean to give up or to quit, it means to stop resisting, to stop fighting against, to stop pushing against. It does not mean just sitting around waiting for things to change. It's acceptance that what is - is and then deciding how to deal with that.

PERFECTIONISM!
THAT'S IT! (BUT NOT REALLY)

Many of us believe that if we can do things perfectly, another form of control, we can lower the chances of disappointment, frustration, and judgment. But we are humans, and perfection isn't a thing that' achievable. It's a form of control, it's holding the elephant on a leash and hoping you look great doing it.

So many of us are perfectionists. Those of you reading who know you are, are keenly aware of it.

And then there are those of you who are like me, who aren't clear on it at all. I was 100% sure I was not a perfectionist. I didn't have to wear the right outfit or get the best grades.

There are so many aspects of my life that I "don't care" or am "whatever" about.

And when it comes down to it, I'm totally a perfectionist. Because in the end, my perfection is more about appearance and the illusion of being cool, calm, collected and accepting of whatever happens. Some people do it with their intelligence or organization. Some do it with sports or their career. I do it through the appearance of "cool".

How are you a perfectionist? Where are you unwilling to surrender and put down all the control you have set up in your life?

What my form of perfection and all other forms have in common is they are living in service of fulfilling an unattainable goal.

Perfectionism, at its core, is about creating an outward appearance of something, beauty, coolness, intelligence, creativity, power, peace, or maybe being right. It is not authentic because it will always be about creating and controlling that appearance for others or beating ourselves up when we aren't 'perfect', or something goes wrong or differently than desired.

Control crushes our dreams. It doesn't allow us to be us. It doesn't allow us to chase the visions, hopes, and goals we have. It creates a culture of people who are afraid to feel, to be ourselves and to even dream about the passions and desire we have. We start creating dreams and goals that are more focused on status, pleasing others, doing what we feel we "should" be doing or is expected of us.

When my coach asked me to surrender, these were the places I was forced to look. Where was I a perfectionist, where was I trying to control circumstances and feelings? Where was I fighting against my feelings or trying to manipulate emotions?

So, I ask you. You can't control life. You can't control the perceptions and feelings of others. With that said, where are you a perfectionist?

Where are you numbing or dampening your emotions?

What do you love that you aren't admitting due to fear?

What passion are you not chasing because of perception, fear or because the circumstances aren't ideal?

Where are you not feeling joy or grateful because you are exacting or waiting for something bad to happen?

YOUR TURN:

1) What are you waiting for? Draft your first Blueprint if you haven't already. Don't limit yourself to circumstances. Really go for it. Accept that you are vulnerable and surrender to putting it all out there. I dare you.

2) How are you a perfectionist? If you put those habits, patterns, and behaviors down, how would life be different?

3) Extra Credit: practice saying the thing that would be most vulnerable for you to share. Notice what happens when you do.

17 | PERSPECTIVE

◆ ◆ ◆

*"The very unfunny cosmic joke: In an attempt to protect
ourselves from pain, we perpetuate behaviors that create
the very pain we are trying to avoid."*

- JEN SINCERO

Bottom line. *Your attitude and perspective shape how you
see the world. This chapter is about:*
- *Understanding that we have perspectives through
  which we see the world that determine how we show
  up*
- *Training our minds to take on perspectives that will
  support us in getting what we want*
- *Cultivating a powerful relationship to practice*

IT'S ALL ABOUT PERSPECTIVE

W e don't want to get our hearts broken so we don't let ourselves open up enough to love someone or be loved by someone.

We don't want to fail, so we don't try or give up.

We don't speak up because we don't want to look bad, stupid, or be told we are wrong.

We don't say I love you first because we might not hear it back.

We don't ask for a raise because we are afraid that we might not get it or worse find out we aren't appreciated at work.

This happens everywhere all the time and it's heartbreaking.

Now how does it relate to attitude?

Our attitude is an exact reflection of the way we see the world, aka our perspective.

Let's take a look: if you view the world as a negative place, how are you going to show up?

Predictably, you may be defensive, protective, or pessimistic. You watch out for what could go wrong, who could fuck up, who will drop the ball, or what might offend someone. You expect negative outcomes.

What changes if instead you view the world as a positive place? You may be the one who always looks for opportunity or believes in the metaphorical light at the end of the tunnel. Predictably, you show up with a sense of optimism, with that belief and hope that everything will work out.

I could create other examples but consider that we as

humans all see the world through particular perspectives. From whichever perspective we see things, we then culti-vate specific attitudes to deal with the world. Our experi-ence of life is a direct reflection of the perspective we have chosen.

I say choose on purpose. While we may have been condi-tioned to see the world through a specific perspective based on how our parents raised us or our community engaged us, as adults we now have the choice and responsibility to de-cide how we look at the world.

There is no right or wrong way to view the world, but I would challenge anyone that says some of the ways aren't vastly more fun, enjoyable, and more fulfilling than others.

The thing about attitude and perspective is that our whole life evolves and grows out of them.

Attitude and perspective are like the vast ocean of our lives. Everything that happens in our lives flows like a river out of that ocean. If the ocean is dirty, the river is dirty. If the ocean is clean the river is clean. If the ocean is filled with possi-bility, the river is going to carry possibility. If the ocean is dried up and empty, then no value can flow from it through the river.

Attitude and perspective, like that ocean, are where we pull from to create our views of the world.

We have control over our attitude and perspective. We can choose to be positive or negative, optimistic or pessimis-tic, or something else. These attitudes and perspectives are not in our DNA. They are learned, and then they become the stories that we tell ourselves over and over again. As children, we pick up on the attitudes and perspectives of those around us and we emulate them. As adults, we have the power to take responsibility for who we are, how we behave, and our behaviors.

When I was a kid I grew up with amazing parents. They saw the world mostly through a perspective of worry. They worried about money, they worried about violence, they worried about my grades, or if I would be good enough to make the baseball team. They worried about cancer, what was in the food we ate, politics, religion, and when the next economic recession would occur.

And remember my parents were amazing. My grandparents were unbelievable. My aunts and uncles were also wonderful. And from my perspective they had all been conditioned to be fearful and worried about negative things happening. My grandparents grew up in climates of The Great Depression and WWII . Then my parents lived through The Cold War, and Vietnam.

If you think about it, they grew up surrounded by scarcity, fear, and not enough. They existed in a world consistently in turmoil, where many faced persecution. So, my grandparents passed on this perspective of fear to my parents. My parents, in turn, taught these things to my brother and me. Our beliefs are conditioned, or even implanted, into our minds. Most of our beliefs come to us through family, friends, society, culture, and possibly religion.

Consider that beliefs work in the following way. A belief is just a thought that we keep thinking. It is not permanent. Our beliefs can get stronger so long as we continue to find evidence to support them. For example, if you believe the world is violent, you will consistently notice all the places where violence takes place. If you believe the world is good, you will more likely notice all the acts of generosity or kindness that happen in the world.

Let's create an example of certain perspectives and beliefs to better see how things play out. Consider that you are a person who perceives life as hard—you have it that things generally don't go your way, and there is always something to deal with at work, with your kids, or with your partner. You also believe money isn't easy to get, and despite having enough of it to live, you believe things should be better. (Wink wink, this is my default perspective, Life is Hard!)

Imagine a typical day in your life as this person. You wake up. Your kids are being fussy and your spouse isn't in the best mood. As you get out of bed, you stub your toe on the foot of the bed. *Shit!* It hurts, but you deal with the pain. You grab your toothbrush and realize that you are out of toothpaste. *Shit!* Now you are hurt, frustrated, cranky, and so is the environment around you.

You leave the house in that state of mind. And you hit every red light on the way to work. Of course! Right?

At work, your boss comes to you pissed off about something that doesn't even have to do with you. A major client cancels a big meeting. Halfway through the day your spouse texts you that the bill is in from the kids' last visit to the doctor, and insurance won't cover it.

This is just life. Events in a day like this one happen, even if they don't necessarily all happen in the same day. And when they happen, they become the evidence that life is always going to be this way. There will always be something. Nothing ever goes your way. Life is hard!

You will filter everything about the world through your attitude, and perspective, or your beliefs. We use these situations and the way we perceive them as evidence to prove to ourselves this is how the world is. And it's not true. When one person gets fired it can be evidence that the world is cruel and that person sucks. Or it can be evidence that they shouldn't have been in that job and there is a better opportunity around the corner.

When good things happen to the person who thinks life is hard, they might even characterize it as lucky and it won't last. We have to have our view of the world match our beliefs. What we see with our eyes and experience has to match the picture of the world in our brains, if it didn't it wouldn't make sense.

Think about someone you know who is negative all the time. Think about how they are when things aren't going well. They are always expecting a disaster or mess of some kind. They even use words and expressions to prove and demonstrate that they are right about how things go. When things go well, they are almost surprised, and believe it's just a matter of time before things change.

Now think of a person that you know to be so positive, you either can't stand how obnoxious you think they are, or you wish you viewed the world like they did. Now don't be shy, we all know someone who's so positive or joyful we can hardly stand to be with them. And if we don't, that person is probably you. (This last statement also applies to the people we hold as negative, if you don't know anyone like that, sorry but it's *you!*)

The super positive and optimistic person you know, expects the best. When good things happen, it's evidence for staying optimistic. When things are negative, they look for the light at the end of the tunnel, or the opportunity in the experience, or maybe they focus on what else in their life is good.

> *"The way you look at life is essentially a barometer of your expectations, based on what you've been taught you're worthy of and capable of achieving."*

> - DR. WAYNE W. DYER

So I have a sucky attitude! I'm negative all the time...so how do I change it?

Great question, Reader.

Don't worry. Just because you grew up in a negative fear-based environment or lived in a country that spoon fed you negativity and fear, does not mean you have to accept it.

You can change your attitude and perspective. Guess how.

Seriously, guess.

It's not a trick question. How do you change it?

Did you guess?

You're probably still reading, waiting for me to tell you. What if I didn't? What if the rest of this book was me just prompting you to guess?

Did you guess yet?

How about now?

How long are we going to do this for?

If you haven't guessed by now, you just aren't fun.

So here we go...

Practice.

That's it. Practice. It's that simple. When you want to change your current skill level at something, you practice. Practice creates the ability to change.

PRACTICE

"Practice is the best of all instructors."

- PUBLILIUS SYRUS

Practice is practice. It doesn't matter if it's a yoga or meditation practice or if you are focusing on being more positive as a practice. Practice is simply focusing on something you want to do different or be different and using focus and repetition to shift it.

When I was a little kid, I was pretty good at basketball. I was fast, strong, and was a good dribbler who could attack the basket in a way in which I could typically score. However, I wasn't so great dribbling with my right-hand. My left-hand was so dominate I typically couldn't get stopped, but I wouldn't let my right-hand practice enough to improve.

I was afraid to use my right as much because I might fail. And in the end, I did fail and couldn't grow as a player because I wasn't good enough with both hands. If I had spent focused time and energy and was willing to be uncomfortable for a while I might have developed more and become a better player.

Practicing at basketball isn't that different from the practice at anything else. Learning to dribble a ball with your non-dominant hand is uncomfortable and awkward at first. When you aren't paying attention, you will always default back to your usual hand. But if you are committed to changing your skills, you would remain conscious of which hand you are dribbling with and continue to use your non-dominant one. This consistence practice is what allows you to improve.

Before we dive into how to practice shifting attitudes and mindsets you might want to ask yourself what is your relationship to practice?

If you aren't sure, how does it go for you when you try new things and want to improve at them?

Do you like practicing things? How do you feel about improving at something slowly overtime?

Do you bear through the difficultly of not being great at something and experience the journey?

Do you focus on the result and judge yourself the entire time? Do you just not do new things because it's too difficult or frustrating?

Finish this sentence.

Practice is ...

I ask my clients to practice things in between every single session.

Why?

Because unless you're a fucking magician, it's literally the only way to improve at anything.

How would you ever expect to change a habit, behavior, or pattern if you aren't willing to practice doing it different? And yet so many of us are unwilling, or don't want to practice. I see it in my business all the time. Clients show up week after week not practicing the things they said they would, the things they said they wanted to grow, change or improve upon.

Unconscious practice is what created the attitude or perspective in the first place. So practicing something new and different is the only way to create a new attitude or perspective.

If you want to change your life, you better get super accustomed to and super comfortable with practicing new things.

For me, my relationship with practice was terrible. It's getting better. I'm practicing.

See what I did there?

Prior to getting involved with coaching, my relationship to practice was pretty messed up.

Remember the lessons from my Fear Stories? I learned I wasn't good enough. See, when you don't think you're good enough, everything becomes about fixing it to be better or avoiding it altogether. It all becomes about performance. When I'm in my Judge mind state, everything is always about performing, everywhere in life. From Judge, if I wasn't the best, I didn't want to do it anymore. Practicing would have required me to be vulnerable and possibly look uncool.

If I wasn't good at something--bowling, golf, computer coding, reading, mediation, ping pong, etc--I didn't do it. I would only do things I was good at. How limiting and lame is that? But I had to keep up that magical image of the cool guy.

When I was introduced to coaching, the idea and concept of taking on practices and practicing without being attached to the results was uncomfortable. Like the many clients I described earlier, I hated it. I had to embrace the catch-22 that it was to say, I wanted to be better at something, yet be unwilling to practice getting better at it. Said another way, I can't get better without practicing, but if I'm unwilling to practice because I'm uncomfortable I can never get better.

"If you want to get good at something, just suck at it fast."

- CHRISTOPHER MCAULIFFE

That is one of my favorite quotes of all time. It's simple and just so real. Basically, what Christopher McAuliffe is saying is if you try and fail at something enough times you will eventually improve. So try and fail faster.

I always think of kids and how they learn to ride bikes. They typically aren't good at it from the get-go. Imagine any kid learning to ride a bike. What happens? They get on, one of their parents runs behind them holding up the bike, and when it seems like the kid has it, the parent lets go.

This kid might stay upright and keep riding, or they make it a few feet and topple over. Even those that stay upright usually have a time when they fall down. They try out rougher terrain. They try out a trick. Maybe they just try stopping and don't have a handle on the breaks. Most kids learning how to ride a bike have moments when they fall. And, most kids who continue to practice riding their bikes, get better at it.

One of the things I love about coaching the way I was trained, is that we work to recreate our relationship to practice. Imagine how many new things you would try if you didn't worry about failing or not being good at it. Think about how many things you would keep doing if you were able to view it from the practice perspective and didn't attach any meaning to how it turned out because it was just practice. So many of us are so averse to failing, to not looking good, many of the things that come with the territory of improvement, that we aren't willing to try them.

Here is an example to highlight why practice matters.
I am working with a client to create a new awareness. He realizes he isn't willing to have the "hard" conversations with his spouse or boss, because he is scared of the response he will get, or the fight that might break out. So, he continues to hold back. He realizes that by continuing to hold back, he suffers in silence. So, while he avoids the fight to avoid suffering, and he just suffers in another way.

Upon getting clear on this, my then client realizes that he holds back everywhere. It is not about his boss or his spouse. It is about him not believing in himself enough to express his voice and ensure his needs are met. Boom! Massive awareness.

From this place, my client sees that he has an attitude and perspective that are no longer working, and he has an opportunity to choose a new way to practice. He could practice speaking up from love or joy, or practice communication as an act of connection. He could simply take on the practice of noticing all of the places in his life he holds back, how often, and then notice the impact on each situation.

When a client sees any new awareness, we quickly want to attach a practice or action to it, with the intention of solidifying that new awareness.

Makes sense? Let's look at another example.

You realize that every time you set the intention of waking up early to work out, you tend to stay up late the night before. You are subconsciously self-sabotaging your goal. In talking about it with your coach, you realize you self-sabotage a lot of your goals because deep down you don't believe you will accomplish them anyway. So instead of trying and failing, you just sabotage so that you don't have to face the fear of possible failure.

So, after you notice this, you might create a practice around it. A great place to start is just by stopping and noticing the next time you are self-sabotaging. Don't judge yourself for it. Just stop and notice and call yourself out on it. Like, "oh, I'm doing that again." Another practice might be to start noticing how often you do it, or in what specific areas of life you do it most.

After you become comfortable with noticing, you can take on a higher-level practice. Challenge yourself to not only notice, but in the moment, pause and make a new choice that would create a new outcome. Don't watch one more sitcom on Netflix. Set your morning alarm. Delete your ex's phone number, Facebook, and Instagram account.

CREATING PRACTICES

Let's bring all of the pieces together.

What practices will support you in having new attitudes and perspectives?

Start with: Notice how this normally goes. That's it. That's a practice. Notice the story you have around how it goes. Notice the meaning you make around and what it means about you.

Acknowledge what perspective that story has trained you to believe.

It's like realizing that money is paper with ink on it. As a society, we have collectively attached a meaning to it and give it power and value. But the physical thing we hold in our hands is just paper with ink on it. The best practice is to notice the meanings we assign.

Another place to look when you want to practice or to try to do things differently, is first choosing how you want something to go.

For example, if you want to change feelings of self-consciousness when doing physical activities. First you notice that you feel uncomfortable exercising, doing yoga, or dancing in front of others. You decide you want to change this and move away from these disempowering self-conscious feelings.

This self-consciousness is limiting. You can start by just noticing. You realize that any time you have a chance to dance or water ski or do anything new these feelings come up. For me when situations like this came up, what I started to notice is that if I wasn't good, it meant something about me as a human being. If people saw me look bad, it would prove I wasn't good enough.

I wanted to generate a practice that would support me in realizing that it was okay not to be great at everything. More importantly, I wanted my perspective to shift such that being good at things or being bad at things didn't matter at all if I wanted to do them. So as a practice I signed up for yoga.

Yes, yoga.

And not just any yoga studio either, an iconic and passion-driven yoga studio, Laughing Lotus in New York City. Looking back, I'm so grateful to them, that studio, and those yogis changed my life.

I digress. For me, going into a yoga class filled with mostly women, mostly very attractive women, was a potentially brilliant idea if the purpose was to simply meet new attractive women. But normally I would never put myself in front of women unless I knew I would look good and having never done yoga before, I probably wasn't going to look good doing any of it.

On top of all of that, vinyasa yoga turned out in its own right to be physically and mentally challenging.

The gift of taking on this particular practice is that yoga is inherently about connecting with yourself in a space outside of overthinking. It challenges you to calm your mind and just be present to everything that is happening. It asks you to not judge yourself, to believe that there is no good or bad, or a place to get to.

My yoga practice served two purposes for me. It meant taking on everything that I mentioned just now; but it also became the place to practice putting down my "cool guy" attitude. It was a place to practice not worrying about how I might look, to simply focus on the movement at hand. It was a practice in not letting my mind take over and convince me that I looked bad or stupid.

Yoga is not the only practice that can create this experience. There are so many physical actives that would push, or challenge someone in this way. I'm simply using yoga as the example, because it was really what I used.

Create a practice right now.

Stumped? Here's a place to start: think of situations or times that you're normally negative. It could be anything. You might be thinking, "I'm never negative, I'm realistic." That works too.

Practice noticing every time you handle a situation from a negative or realistic perspective.

After you've gotten facility with noticing how often and in what situations you're doing it, then you can take on another practice trying to distinguish why you might be doing that. What's underneath the need to be negative or realistic? After that you might create a practice that asks you to notice, and then be intentional about looking for the opportunity inside of the challenge.

Now, create the practice.

Nice work!

THE GIVING ATTITUDE

"No one has ever become more poor by giving."

- ANNE FRANK

To close out this chapter, I want to address an attitude shift that is paramount in reaching your goals.

I'm going to share something with you now that might mess with your head. You might need to read this a few times. It doesn't have to do with your intelligence, it's simply not what we've spent our lives learning.

So here goes.

When you are wanting something, you are in a state of not having it.

Read it again.

When you *want* something and you focus on *wanting* it, you are subconsciously and energetically putting your attention on *not having* it.

Makes sense, right? If you want something, you don't have it, so by focusing on what you want you are also focused on what you don't have. #mindfuck

That's messed up right?

So how do we avoid subconsciously pushing what we want further and further away from ourselves?

The answer is actually quite simple.

Gratitude and Giving!

But how do you have gratitude when things aren't going well?

How do you give when you don't think you have enough?

I'm not suggesting that Gratitude and Giving will just make your life perfect. I'm not proposing that just smiling and being grateful is going to solve all your problems. But from my own practice, I guarantee that when you shift your attitude to Gratitude and Giving, your life has a way of shifting.

Let's look at each individually.

"I am happy because I'm grateful. I choose to be grateful. That gratitude allows me to be happy."

- WILL ARNETT

Let's try something right now. Grab a pen. Let's make a list of things you can be grateful for.

This can be anything. You can be grateful that you have food or that you woke up today. You can be grateful for your cellphone or TV, the oxygen you breathe or the water you drink. You can be grateful for relatives, your job, or if you hate your job, the money it pays you. You can be grateful for the flowers you saw on your way to work, the parents you had growing up, refrigeration, beer, your favorite shoes, your friends or even French fries. You can be grateful for your yoga practice, morning coffee, this book, your bed, or even sleep!

Seriously, you can be grateful for anything and we all have something. Nelson Mandela endured 27 years in prison and throughout learned to love those who imprisoned him, found things to be grateful for, and found places to look to identify love and humanity.

While we aren't all Nelson Mandela or striving to be, it's simply an example of what's possible.

None of us are the first to suffer. None of us are the first to endure hardships, challenges or struggle. We don't have to be grateful for whatever we are enduring, but we can look around and find things for which we can be grateful.

So, look around, take stock of your life. I assert things could be even worse than they are. And they could be better. But what can you be grateful for today? Can you come up with five things right now?

Go!

If you didn't already, can you go back and add why you are grateful for those things?

For instance, I'm grateful for the sun on my face because it feels good. It also supports the growing of plants that produce oxygen for us and food. Also, it gives me Vitamin D.

"Gratitude makes sense of our past, brings peace for today, and creates a vision for tomorrow."

- MELODY BEATTIE

Forbes published an article stating all the health benefits of gratitude. Here's what they found:

1) According to a 2014 study published in Emotion, gratitude improves relationships and can create new opportunities.

2) According to a 2012 study published in Personality and Individual Differences grateful people take better care of themselves and their health.

3) According to Dr. Robert A. Emmons studies gratitude improves psychological health increasing happiness and reducing depression.

4) According to a 2012 study by University of Kentucky those who ranked higher on gratitude scores experienced more sensitivity and empathy towards others and less of a desire for revenge.

5) According to a 2011 study published in Applied Psychology: Health and Wellness those who wrote down a few things to be grateful for before bed sleep better and longer.

6) According to a 2014 study published in Journal of Applied Sports Psychology gratitude increased athletes self-esteem contributing to optimal performance as well as diminishing social comparisons a major factor in resentment.

7) According to a 2006 study published in Behavior Research and Therapy showed that those with higher levels of gratitude experienced lower rates of PTSD.

8) And a 2003 study published in Journal of Personality and Social Psychology showed that gratitude was a major factor contributing to resilience following 9/11.

If you typed into your search bar "gratitude research," you would be bombarded with an array of research on the topic. Most sources agree, the key factor to leading a fulfilling life of joy is gratitude. Shifting your attitude to one of Gratitude (even without rhyming it) will allow you to remain focused on what is working in your life and create productivity to grow the areas of your life into more of what you want.

I practice gratitude daily. I do two things. One, during my morning ritual, I write down three things I'm grateful for and why. Two, throughout the day when I notice I'm judging another or simply thinking negatively, I practice generating something I can be grateful for in regard to the person or situation. Another practice I take on is looking for the gift in a person or situation that I'm relating to negatively or judgmentally. If I'm feeling like I don't have enough money to buy something I want, I might pause and think about what opportunity exists, potentially the motivation to earn more money or I might notice all the space that exists in my bank account waiting to be filled. I know that may sounds silly, but we can do this anywhere and in any situation.

If you're skeptical, I only suggest you start and see for yourself what a simple gratitude practice opens up for you. Start with listing three things you can be grateful for and why in the morning or night or both. Commit to the practice for 30 days and at the end of the 30 days, notice what is different in your life.

"Happiness is not a goal, it's a byproduct."

- ELEANOR ROOSEVELT

Have you ever met a hoarder? I have and I've seen the show.

What do you think of when you see someone hoarding? What do you imagine or wonder about their mindset, their life, or their attitude?

What do we know about hoarders?

Well we know they are fearful, worried, anxious and afraid. We know that at some level they live inside a scarcity, meaning a mindset of not enough. We know that all these things might not be conscious also. What's clear on the surface is they can't seem to part ways with anything for fear that they might need it, want it or won't be able to get it again.

I don't know about you, but I've never seen a happy, successful, joyous hoarder enjoying the magnificence of their lives. I've also never met a hoarder who was all about giving, the two just don't go together.

What I love about the concept of giving is that you can't give something you don't have.
If we think we don't have, we can't give. If we have, but are afraid we cannot replace, we can't give. If we are fearful there isn't enough, we can't give.

But we live in an abundance-rich world. We have been taught lies of scarcity, that there isn't enough and that we must take, take, take. But it's not true. While there are things that are scarce it is humans that have made it so.

There is enough food for everyone but we, based on financial markets and monetary prioritization, choose not to enable everyone to eat. There is enough money for everyone to have some, but we have chosen a system that allows some to live in excess while others live in poverty. There is enough clean air, but we have polluted the air and cut down the trees that would create new oxygen.

I could go on and on. We have so much. Start looking around. There is a choice to be made when you do. You can look at the excess or you can look at scarcity, it's just a choice as to what perspective you choose to see the world.

Now if we have enough, what or why would we want to give?

Giving opens us up, it creates space for something new, more, a change, the things that we want.

Giving tells the universe and our subconscious that we have enough to give away and share. It's a deliberate action that indicates abundance, and when we are in the attitude of abundance, we can create more, grow and generate more of what we want. If we are in the attitude of scarcity, that there isn't enough, it makes it tough to create or generate what we want because you cannot create something you don't think exists or think isn't possible.

A few years ago, I was vacationing in Folly Beach, South Carolina. If you haven't been, what an amazing beach town. I highly recommend visiting.

One morning my then-girlfriend and I were grabbing a morning coffee and an early breakfast pastry. Folly Beach is a beach town, so on most early days the town is calm, quiet, and peaceful. That morning a local was getting his coffee. As we were eating and drinking, we heard that he didn't have his wallet.

Most of us have lived this moment. It's awkward. We get all sorts of anxiety and start our version of panic. I don't know why, or what compelled me, but I turned around and offered to buy his coffees for him. He and the cashier were both surprised. He offered to get his wallet and come back, which wasn't necessary.

The purchase itself wasn't a huge deal, it was only a few dollars. But this act of giving had an unintended "consequence" for me. All day I felt a little happier than normal, because of a few dollars I gave away. And all day, I knew that this guy was a little happier because some random person did something nice for him. Some random person simply made his day a little easier.

My girlfriend and I wondered if he paid it forward later or with someone else. Did he share the story with another, did they pay it forward? It didn't actually matter, what mattered was we felt good about what we did and that wasn't even the intention. Giving and doing kind generous things for others makes us feel good, which implies we should be doing more of it.

When I think back to that moment, I was in the beginnings of building my new coaching practice. I didn't have many clients, I didn't make enough money to cover my own bills and expenses yet. If I had paused, I might have thought that I didn't have enough money to be giving some away. And with that attitude, I would have been subconsciously confirming the lack in my life. I would have been living in the present from lack and creating the future from lack. What I subconsciously did was create from the future I wanted to build, which was one of giving.

Recently someone said to me if you can't give 10% of $1,000, you won't be able to give 10% of $1,000,000. And that is so true. We think that at a certain point we'll have enough. But giving isn't about having. It's about attitude and believing in abundance and generosity.

Giving makes us happier. A study by scientists in Zurich reported that people's happiness levels increased after acts of generosity. The scientists stated:

> *"Generosity and happiness improve individual well-being and can facilitate societal success... However, in everyday life, people underestimate the link between generosity and happiness and therefore overlook the benefits..."*

I want to issue a challenge. You get to set the parameters, but it's a "giving" challenge none the less.

For the next 30 days, give something. I don't care what you give or how much but give something every day. That might mean a donation to a charity. It might mean money to the homeless person who you see standing at the freeway on-ramp every day on your way to work. It might mean buying the person behind you coffee or paying the toll for the car behind you. It might mean giving a hug or support or dropping off old clothes at Goodwill. It might mean calling someone up and sharing your love for them. It might mean giving forgiveness or gratitude to another. It doesn't matter but give something.

While you are giving, notice how it feels. Don't give for the feeling, but just notice. Give to clear the space, give to invite more in, give because you are abundant and because we are all human beings and to give to another is a way of sharing your love and connection.

YOUR TURN:

1) Identify 3 perspectives you currently have, and how they are getting in the way of your goals.

2) Create a structure to hold you accountable to the practices you generated. Is it scheduling alarms in your phone? Writing a reminder on your bathroom mirror? Create whatever it is now.

3) Commit to taking on my Gratitude Challenge and Giving Challenge.

18 | SUPPORT

◆ ◆ ◆

"Each person holds so much power within themselves that needs to be let out. Sometimes they just need a little nudge, a little direction, a little support, a little coaching, and the greatest things can happen."

- PETE CARROLL

Bottom line. *Nobody does anything powerful, life changing, or magnificent alone If you want to go big go together. This chapter is about:*

· *Defining support*

· *Identifying the areas of our lives where we need support*

· *Underscoring what's possible if we get the support that we need*

WHAT IS SUPPORT?

What does support mean to you?

To me, the words support and help used to mean the same thing—and help was annoying. You can't do it yourself, so get help. You aren't good enough, so get help. Help was just a reminder that there were things I couldn't do, and if I couldn't do them myself then I wasn't good enough. Support was just a kinder, gentler, and softer way of saying get some help.

I distinctly remember being in my twenties and helping a friend move from one apartment to another. I thought to myself, after twenty-five I'm not going to help anyone move anymore and nobody better ask. I was pretty set in my righteous belief that at twenty-five you better have your shit together enough that you can hire movers.

Basically, in my mind, if you were over twenty-five and couldn't pay to have someone move you, you sucked and didn't have your shit together. And you shouldn't bother asking me for help.

Yes, I was a dick.

Since we've talked a lot about beliefs and attitudes so far, let's dissect some of mine from this story. First, not paying for a mover means you suck at life, since you aren't successful enough to afford it. Second, by the age of twenty-five you should no longer need to your friends for this type of help anymore and should be able to afford it.

On the flip side, if my parents offered me any financial support, I would have gladly accepted it. Free money from Mommy and Daddy didn't equate to failure but not being able to hire movers did. I throw in this example to put to how contradictory we can all be in our beliefs.

These contradictions and conditions showed up for me everywhere around support.

I would ask for editing support when I was writing. But if the person supporting me gave me too many notes of feedback, I'd get upset and frustrated.

At work, I had no problem giving and receiving help from anyone. But outside of work, if someone needed my help, especially physical help with something, they better have been a very attractive woman, or I wasn't interested.

I'm not sharing this so you can see how much of an asshole I was, but to point out that support shows up in various ways and we all relate to it differently. Support is emotional, physical, financial, or spiritual. It can be temporary or long-term. It may require action, or it simply requires listening or being with another person.

What is your relationship to support? Think about it. If Support was a person in your life—especially your partner or co-worker—how would you describe your relationship to support?

What do you notice?

How is that relationship going?

Here are a few more questions you might ask yourself:

Where are you under supported?
Where are you overly supported?
In what areas of your life do you ask for support?
In what areas of life do you avoid support?
Where could you use support currently in your life? Who would you ask? What do you need from them?

Now we are going to take a look at the various areas of your life. Take a moment and grade how much support you could use in each on a scale of A-F, F being needing it the most.

Relationship
Errands and To Do's
Work
Physical/Exercise
Emotional
Spiritual
Educational
Medical
Childcare

Look at each of the categories, what is one way you could ask for support in each? Think about the thing that could raise your grade by one letter? What is the one thing you could ask for? Who could you ask?

Jot it down.

Cool, are you willing to follow through with that step towards getting more supported? If not, what is stopping you? Might be a great conversation to have with a therapist or a coach?

For some of you, this might be too much already. Many of us have a disempowered relationship to support. I know I did.

I was never great at asking for help. It always felt like a weakness.

I didn't know how to get my needs met. I didn't even know what to say when someone asked me, "what do you need?"

Getting supported and not going through life alone is one of the keys to create a life that works. Nobody does anything great all by themselves. Everyone has a team, a community, a group, a family or some support structure. And while most of us have it, we still don't know how to or are unwilling to utilize it.

"The only mistake you can make is not asking for help."

- SANDEEP JAUHAR

I despise the term, "self-made man" because nobody is self-made. No person did it all by themselves. They may have started with nothing, they may have not been handed anything. But everyone has a team, advisors, support, mentors, assistance, colleagues, friends, family, and/or followers.

Everyone has help somewhere along the way. Those of us that create something all on our own still built or created on the backs of others that came before us, and likely others supported us in sharing it or getting it out into the world.

I say this as so many of us are averse to getting supported. Many of us don't know how to get supported. We don't know what to ask for, don't know what we need, and don't know how to receive.

While this seems so simple, this is an area of growth for most human beings. If we could get supported, how much healthier would we be? How much less stress would we feel? How much further would we or our ideas go? How much more love would we have? How much more held and cherished would our children feel?

Being supported by someone can change your life.

DON'T FORGET TO GIVE

We've been talking a lot about getting support, but what about giving support?

"If you're not making someone else's life better, then

you're wasting your time. Your life will become better by making other lives better."

What does giving support look like for you?

Do you avoid it at all costs?

Do you live to support others, putting your needs before theirs?

List at least five people you know you could (and possibly would even like to) be supporting right now.

What is stopping you from supporting them?

What action will you take to start support each of the people above?

WHAT SUPPORT MAKES POSSIBLE

When I decided I wanted to change my life, I took on a few different structures of support; the first structure was I told a lot of people. I told everyone I could in fact. In doing so I had public accountability.

For instance, if you decided to become a vegetarian and told everyone you knew, then the next time you tried ordering a burger, those with you would likely ask about the vegetarian thing.

While you can do whatever you want, if you use public accountability you are going to have to answer some questions. For some of us that is enough.

Another thing I did was I started to reach out to people whose lives I was envious of and started asking them questions. They had clearly created a life that I wanted, I imagined they knew something I didn't.

In just opening that door and calling people, I was pointed in various directions, given advice, acknowledged, encouraged, and inspired. Through one of those conversations I learned more about network marketing and sales. While this wasn't the direction I'd ultimately go in, I learned a lot about personal growth, sales, networking and team building.

Through network marketing I was also introduced to BNI, Business Networking International, a wonderful networking group and global community. And if it hadn't been for BNI I might have never met a coach.

When I started attending BNI meetings I started to meet people in all sorts of professions, some were careers I was familiar with, others I'd never heard of. The first time I met a "coach" or "life coach" I was very confused. I didn't understand how someone could be so positive, so full of life and see possibility everywhere. It all seemed fake to me. After a few short months I had met a handful of coaches and was very curious about what they did, if it worked and what could I get out of a coaching session.

Now it wasn't until I met my seventh coach (yes, seventh) that I said yes to a Sample Session. A sample session is typically a free coaching session to give a potential client or interested person a taste of what coaching is, what the process looks like and have an idea of how coaching can add power and velocity into their life.

That sample session cracked me wide open. I was able to see that it was my actions, behaviors and decisions that created the life I was living, that it wasn't anyone else's fault. I saw that only I was responsible for my life. More so, I realized I wanted to be a coach. I wanted to support others like I experienced in that first coaching session.

Getting supported was like reopening doors of possibility and opportunity that I had once been closed off to.

It's pretty amazing to think that if I hadn't opened up to reading, network marketing, BNI or all the other things I tried through asking for and getting supported, I might have never met coaches. And if that hadn't happened, who knows if I would have ever transformed my life, changed my relationship to myself and others, created a pretty wonderful life, or have become a coach myself.

Shit maybe I wouldn't be writing this book.

There's a real possibility that I'd still be in the hospitality business, drinking too much, spending money buying things for moments of happiness, living for days off, vacations and other ego-driven endeavors.

Let's look at other ways I've gotten supported over the last few years.

When I decided I wanted to be a coach, I knew I needed training and structure. Accomplishment Coaching's Coach & Leadership Training Program is the best in the world. At the time I wanted to register for it, it cost more money than I had sitting around. I could have just charged it, but I didn't think that was a smart idea.

I also could have let money stop me from taking the next step. So many of us do that. We want something and use money as a cop out. Sorry to break it to you but if you want it badly enough you will find a way.

Now, we all have different resources, different opportunities, different strengths, different weaknesses. But the thing we don't think about as often is, are we willing to ask for help.

For me, I wanted this particular program. And I was willing

to ask my parents for the financial support. If you read that and think that you would never ask your parents, or anyone, for financial help, that's fine. You don't have to.

But do you stop there? Do you not get the thing you want because you have some story about asking people for money? There is no right or wrong way to get supported, but we often stop at asking for the support we are comfortable with.

I was lucky, and I also had spent years cultivating a great relationship with my parents. Reaching out and asking them for financial support wasn't that challenging, even though I didn't know if they would actually say yes.

I called my parents, I shared with them what I was up to, what I wanted to do and what was stopping me.

And I asked them for help!

Now for some of you reading this, this is a big deal, right? You would never! For some of you, asking a parent for help isn't an option, or your parents couldn't help you out, and there are those of us who wouldn't ask for help no matter what.

I've actually had clients who've told me they'd starve before they ask their parents for money.
Now it's not for me to judge what you will or won't do but starving over asking for help isn't serving you or your goals, its ego running the show.

I recently had a client who wanted to hire me. He was stopped by the cost. It wasn't that it was so "expensive" he said, it was that he was saving for a big real estate purchase and didn't want to take any money away from that. He saw the value, but he just didn't know where to get the money from. At the end of our sample session he created a few practices to create the money.

The amazing thing that happened was within ten minutes of getting off the phone he texted me that he talked to his boss and his company was going to pay for it. That wasn't even one of the ideas we created.

It's amazing how when we want something badly enough and are willing to figure out a way, we do.

I had some ego around asking for my parents also. I always thought that by the time I was in my thirties, I would have the money to buy my parents a house or take them on vacation. I never expected I'd be asking them for money.

For me the challenge was internal. Asking was challenging because I made myself wrong for it and I made it mean that I sucked. While I know all this is made up, that's what was going on in my head. But I'm so grateful I had the courage to ask them anyway as that decision changed my life.

It's ironic, as I wrote the first draft of this chapter, I was sitting in my parents' backyard, getting supported by them once again.

At the start of 2017, I ended an engagement. My former fiancée is wonderful woman, and I can't say enough kind things about her. As fortune would have it, it simply didn't work out. The breakup wasn't easy. Ending the relationship was the hardest thing I've ever done. I loved her, and I knew it was going to kill and tear both of us apart...and I also knew it was the right thing to do.

After the breakup and moving out of our place in New York, I had nowhere to go.

I was in the first year of my coaching practice, and I didn't have the money to both give my ex a few months advance for the rent I was walking out of and start paying for a place of my own. On top of that, I didn't want to live in NYC anymore.

I did two things.

I asked a friend to come help me pack up my stuff, which he did. I will forever be grateful for that, because I don't know how I would have done it alone. I was heartbroken, packing up was like digging ditches while crying.

There was a part of me that would have preferred to do it alone. That part would have been ashamed of the tears, not wanting another person to see them, especially another man.

There was a part of me that felt guilty about asking for help, like who would want to help me.

Remember my thing about moving? Asking someone to help me pack up and move boxes was lame and not worth their time.

It took realizing that asking for help was human, that asking for support was a need and by not asking I was only punishing myself more.

The second thing I did was even more challenging for my ego.

I called my parents. While my parents are crazy supportive, loving and totally have my back, I was in my thirties, and calling my parents for help just felt lame and had loser written all over it.

So, in my head I put my tail between my legs and asked for support. This time I didn't need money, but I needed a place to crash, a place to store my stuff, a place to get love and supported. I needed a place to go lick my wounds and heal.

Asking them for support was hard. The Hater in my head was loving it, what a loser I was, he would say. I must really suck to be living, even though it was just for a moment, with my parents. What kind of coach could I be if this what my situation? He ate it up and beat me with it. And my Wimp was believing every word.

It wasn't until after a conversation with my coach that I was able to see that this is one of the most powerful ways we get supported, going home. We get loved. We get to heal, and patch ourselves up so we can come back stronger than ever.

How lucky was I to have a home to go to? To have parents that would be there? To have a family that would love me and support me back to full strength?

Having support is one of the most impactful and important things we can do for ourselves. Besides the relationship I've created with my parents, I've also set up some pretty powerful support structures in other areas of my life.

There are so many other friends who loved me and supported me during that difficult time, you know who you are, thank you and I'm so grateful.

I have close colleagues that I text with daily to support me emotionally with all that comes with being an entrepreneur. We talk, text, share, rally each other, give and get advice, and really pick each other up after tough times and losses.

I also have a coach who I can bring anything to. I know that no matter what they will love me, and only stand and see me in my greatness. I have daily calls with other colleagues who are working on projects and during those calls we put each other on mute and spend the time working on the thing we avoid but are committed to completing.

This book literally wouldn't be getting finished if it weren't for me asking for support.

What value do you see in getting supported?

What would an increased level of support bring to your life?

If you haven't already identified areas in which you need support, are you willing to do that now?

Go ahead, we all need support, it actually makes you brave to own it and acknowledge it.

SO WHAT DOES IT LOOK LIKE?

What might that support look like?

Take the next few moments to create ways, there are no wrong ways, to get the support you need.

I provided a few examples through my journey, but here are a few more ideas.

If you feel you are lacking love or emotional connection, from who will you get it? What does receiving love or emotional connection even look like for you?

Be specific when asking. If you tell your friend or family member you need some support and you need love, they might not know what that means or provide it in a way that doesn't help you. Don't assume love or support means the same thing to everyone. A great resource around this topic is Gary Chatman's The 5 Love Languages, a book which breaks down how different types of people give and receive love.

The point is to be specific. Do you want them to just listen? Do you need a hug, a gift, quality time, or some acknowledgment? Do you want someone to have fun with?

Maybe you need support or an accountability buddy to help you get to the gym. Who might you ask? Why would they be a good support system? How do you want them to support you? What might be in it for them?

If you want to lose weight and it's not just exercise but eating better that you need support with here are some ways to create structure. You might write on the top of your shopping list to only buy healthy items. You might ask the person you live with or your partner to remind you that you are trying to eat healthy and to speak if they see you reaching for extra sugar. You might put photos of the body you want on your refrigerator to stop you from eating in a way that won't help you get that result. You might even craft rewards for sticking to the plan or consequences for breaking it.

DISCLAIMER

Now there's one other thing to remember around support. Let's not just sling out crap at someone else. It's not my parents' job to let me crash, it's definitely not their job to give me money.

It's not anyone's job to love you, or hug you, or remind you to workout. I share this because it's not anyone's job you want to make it mutually beneficial for both of you to be supporting each other. You might get support at times from those people who want you to win or love you and other times you might want to create ways that you can support them in return.

Lastly, it's important you remember, it's still your responsibility to get to the gym, it's still mine to be a good house guest and make sure for how long I'm welcome. Be responsible with how you ask for support and how you receive it.

Take the next few minutes and decide how you will get your support needs met.

YOUR TURN:

1) What are you waiting for? Come up with 5 areas of your life where you could use support.

2) Create what you will take on, and what structures you will put in place to follow through.

3) If you have not already, come up with 5 people you could offer support to. Plan by when you will do so. Remember, giving shifts your perspective in an empowered way.

19 | TRUST & FAITH

◆ ◆ ◆

"You must not lose faith in humanity. Humanity is an ocean; if a few drops of the ocean area dirty, the ocean does not become dirty."

Bottom line. *Transformation work will open up your relationship to trust and faith, whether you like it or not. This chapter is about:*
- *Separating Trust & Faith from Religion or whatever else we were raised with*
- *Understanding our current relationships to Trust and to Faith*
- *Seeing how the two are deeply connected*

SPIRITUALITY/GOD/RELIGION/
THE UNIVERSE/ENERGY/
OR WHATEVER YOU WANT
TO CALL...

"Faith is taking the first step even when you don't see the whole staircase."

When I started my journey in personal development and transformation, I had zero connection to God, Spirit, The Universe, or something larger.

I'm serious. Zero connection. If we had met and you told me you believed in God, I likely would have told you that you were an idiot who was falling for the greatest scam of all time.

I wish I could say this was an exaggeration. Or maybe I don't because it truly shows how far I have come. And I say, I wish, because I offended and hurt a lot of people's feelings and I just wasn't nice. I also wasn't able to engage in conversation around the topic because I was so highly triggered and righteous about it.

So, what changed?

As my journey of transformation began, I was forced, because I chose to change things, to look at all areas of my life. I use "forced" loosely as it was clearly a choice of mine at the end of the day.

In the various areas of my life I looked at why I felt certain ways, and where those feelings evolved from. How they got developed. Where was I currently choosing from? Were my choices or beliefs simply auto-pilot or was I creating them? Why was I so triggered around religion, God, and spirituality?

As I pondered these questions, I knew I needed to look at this area.

Some of you are staring at this page, saying to yourself, "really, why does this even matter?" Or having thoughts that are even more anti this conversation.

Maybe you are still holding on to opinions of God or Religion like I was from my youth and believe that those who believe in God or follow religion are (your judgements here).

Others of you reading this are so happy we finally got to the part about faith and can't wait to see how trusting in God fits into the plan.

Maybe some of you don't have an opinion one way or the other when it comes to this topic.

Before we dive into this chapter, I want to state very clearly, I'm not attached to what you believe. What I am interested in is supporting you around opening your mind, your heart and your spirit to the conversation so you can make powerful choices that are not solely based on what your family, community or society imposed on you.

This isn't about changing your beliefs, faith or religion. It's simply about looking at where they came from, whether they are empowered or disempowered, and whether you are powerfully choosing them to support your life.

What I would like to start with is breaking down God, The Universe, or whatever you think of as the divine higher power as separate from Religion.

For clarity's sake, and for this conversation, let's hold that religion has been man's way to create structure and organization around the idea of God. Often what we think of as religions have rules, specific practices, hierarchies, leaders, and places of worship. This isn't good or bad, it's just what religion is.

Spirituality could be viewed as one's personal connection to something larger than ourselves.

And yes, it can embody religion and it often also has no connection to a religion.

God, The Universe, Jesus, Nature, Krishna, Energy, a Disney Minion or whatever you want to call your higher power is your choice, and for this conversation we will simply call God, God. I like first names, it's just easier.

I've set out these definitions because I want us to be clear on where I am speaking from. I've included this chapter because too often many of us are not having conversations about God from a clear and empowered place. Many of us have not powerfully chosen to believe what we believe from an authentic place in our hearts and core.

So, before we go forward are you willing to be open, put down what you know, what you think you know, what you are attached to and simply be here reading this with an observant mind?
The key to transformation is a willingness to look at everything in our lives. For one reason or another, this is often an area where we get especially triggered. Are you willing to simply observe your own thoughts, your reactions, your feelings?

Let's look at me as an example, as it's always a wonderful place to excavate.

In the earlier years of my life, religion was forced upon me, and I hated it. I didn't believe in God and I've already shared my harsh opinions for those that did. If you couldn't prove it to me, it was nonsense. I never even thought about spirituality as something separate from religion. For me for as far back as I can remember, it was all a bunch of crap.

Even into my twenties and early thirties, if you asked me to go to a Church, Temple or any house of worship with you, I would have scoffed and likely belittled you about your beliefs.

Yes, I was a righteous asshole.

In an earlier chapter I mentioned my former fiancée. While it didn't work out, one reason I hold our relationship in a special place in my heart is because I believe it pushed me to grow in ways beyond my wildest dreams.

I often think of that relationship, which lasted almost my entire span of living in New York City, as a cocoon of my transformation. I wouldn't be who I am today if it had not been for the love and support of that woman, and the relationship we created. I will always be grateful.

I share this because as our relationship was getting more serious, an area we often would fight or face challenges around was around religion. She was very connected to and loved her family's beliefs and culture.

I loved culture, especially when it came to finding out where the best foods came from. But religion I had zero space for. We would simply trigger each other back and forth. She'd invite me to something religious and I'd make a rude comment. Sometimes I would participate and end up making jokes the entire time. I frankly, more often than not, was acting like a child, who instead of dealing with my discomfort, made jokes.

As I said before, I loved her. I wanted our relationship to work. I saw a future with her. I saw a family, and for her that included religion and her family's culture. But for me religion kept getting in the way.

I wasn't interested in going to any church or raising my kids with any religion. It was a total hard stop. But because I loved her and was committed to the relationship, I was open to getting support around why I was so triggered around it all.

One day I had a conversation with one of my coaching colleagues about it. She asked me a lot of questions around why I was so unwilling to shift even if it might cost us the relationship. At first, we weren't getting anywhere. I was righteous and had to stand my ground.

Then, she asked me, "What is the age of this conversation?"

It's a weird question, right? What it means is, what is the age of the person who you are being who's having the conversation.

And this is where I saw something powerful.

What I noticed was the conversation I was having wasn't one of an adult man. I was relating to the situation through the lens of "Alex The Seven-Year-Old."

Like most kids, I didn't get much of a say around religion and traditions and I wasn't interested in any of it. From a very young age I didn't connect with religion and at that time I also didn't believe in God. While my parents did their best, they had to force me to do the religious things that I wasn't at all interested in.

To me, I was forced against my will to do things I didn't believe in. As a kid I felt I had little to no say over my own life and beliefs. And frankly for me it went deeper than that.

As I've shared before I was obsessed with being the "cool kid." I didn't believe being Jewish (as my Mom is) or being raised as Jewish would help me be "cool". I was frankly embarrassed and ashamed, not for anything real, but because it didn't seem cool to my little kid brain.

As a kid, I didn't know how to articulate that. But I did know how to kick and scream and push it all away.

Please realize, all that I just shared is very distinguished from my adult brain. As a kid I just felt forced by my parents and not cool. And I see as an adult my parents were doing the best they could.

When I grew up, I was still holding all that energy from the past. I had never taken a new look at religion or God from any lens but the lens of my childhood.

How crazy is that?

How many of us are walking around with thoughts and opinions about all sorts of things simply from the lens and beliefs we created as kids?

While I didn't realize I was relating to it in this way, it became apparent when my colleague pointed it out in that conversation. (I love coaching for this reason, I might have never seen it without that question).

Realizing that I was letting seven-year-old Alex "drive the bus" of my religious beliefs and opinions, was crazy and I knew it wasn't serving me. We wouldn't let a seven-year-old drive any kind of bus and we surely wouldn't trust a seven-year-old to make decisions for us or set the tone for how we should act, behave or live.

But I was.

I was letting a seven-year-old take over anytime God or Religion came up in my life. This wasn't working for me, my life or my relationship. I could absolutely choose the same option to hate Religion and not believe in God, if that's what I wanted, but I could do it from the present space.

This would require me looking at how my beliefs and opinions were formed and who I was being when I was showing up in these conversations.

I think you get the point.

So where are you doing this? It might be around God, Religion or Spirituality, but it might also be in a bunch of other places.

And I don't care what you believe around God, Religion or Spirituality. I do want you to be able to choose powerfully and create structures for you to make the choices from an empowered place that has you leaving the past in the past.

It's called the past for a reason.

The reason I started this chapter on trust and faith with God is that it's hard to have trust or faith without believing in something larger. Again, it doesn't have to be God, it could be Mother Nature or Energy.

The reason it's tough to have trust or faith without having a larger belief is, what would one have trust or faith in? Yes, you can have trust or faith in yourself. Yet, from that place you are implying that you are all you have to count on, and seriously, that's a lot to put on one human.

It's likely that many of you are agreeing or disagreeing with me. And that's okay. I would love to invite you into the conversation that does not include agreeing or disagreeing.

See with agree/disagree, the conversation can only take two directions. We fight and argue until neither of us are convinced, or we stop because we agree. Maybe we stop at agreeing to disagree.

But regardless the conversation doesn't' move forward. Remind you of anything... Politics maybe. When nothing ever gets solved or changes, everything is operating from agree or disagree and right or wrong. It's just a tennis match of back and forth.

I'm sure you see this a lot with religious conversations as well. We are all looking to agree or disagree. By inviting you to not agree or disagree I'm asking you to take it all in. Let it sit, try looking at it in your own life and see what you see or even write down what you hear.

What's great about it is in the end you might still disagree or agree, but you also might see something new for yourself. What shows up doesn't have to change or shift your opinion but it might just open up your perspective. Who doesn't want more perspective to work with?

What's cool about what I believe now is that it came together through deep introspection, deep soul searching, mediation, journeys, reiki, yoga and a lot of reading. I had to put down my conditioning and really get out of my own way and create something totally new.

I realized that I do believe in God/The Universe/Energy. I believe that there is something bigger at play, something that isn't judging us or wanting us to do or be anything other than what we want for ourselves.

Why this is important for you?

Take a look at what you believe. Where do those beliefs came from? Are they yours? Your family's? Your community's?

Are they empowering? Do you just believe what you believe because you were told or conditioned to do so?

Answering these questions myself is how I started my conversation with Trust and Faith.

TRUST & FAITH

Trusting and having faith are critical in deconstructing the fictional life you created and building the life you want. Trust and Faith will support you in standing tall as the person you know yourself to be.

So, what is your relationship to God or whatever you call it? Where did these beliefs come from? Did you ever choose them or just adopt what you were given? Are you happy with those beliefs and do they support the life you want to create?

What is your relationship to Faith? What does having faith mean to you? What do you have faith in?

What is your relationship to Trust? Who do you trust? How do you trust? What does trust in your world look like?

Answer those questions as deeply and thoroughly as you need to. You might go sit somewhere quiet, play light music, meditate first or just watch nature. Regardless, take a bit of time to look at where your beliefs came from, how they evolved and how they impact you now.

TRUST

Let's dive into Trust.

I want to challenge you on something. The way you currently decide who to trust and who not to trust does not only doesn't work, it makes very little sense.

My guess is you don't like that statement and want to know where I'm going from here.

So, let's think about how you trust people. How does it normally go?

What I've learned is that we fall into two camps. Either we trust people right away, or we don't.

For those in the 'trust right away' camp, we start by trusting people and then at some point, those people do something to mess up and break that trust.

For those in the 'don't' camp, we start by making people earn our trust. And guess what, eventually those people also do something to mess up and break that trust.

So regardless of which camp we are in, neither really works.

Maybe you have your own special camp. You truly don't trust anyone, ever. How's that going for you?

My assertion is that with the current way you play the trust game, I believe you aren't winning at it.

What might it look like to win at the trust game?

It starts with trust in ourselves. If we can't trust ourselves, how can we bring that to others?

We can't.

So how do you start having trust in yourself?

Start by first taking a look at where you don't trust yourself. Consider that for most of us, our relationship in this area with ourselves is pretty poor.

How many promises have you broken to yourself? Have you promised you would start a diet, but always put it off? Did you declare you would write a book, but found reason to be too busy?

We have all broken promises to ourselves. All of us. As we break more of these promises, we start to distrust ourselves. We may not think of it as distrust. But ultimately, we are slowly losing belief in ourselves.

What are five areas in your life where you don't trust yourself?

And now where do you have trust in yourself? Again, come up with five areas.

Great. Nice job being honest with yourself. We need to start building up the relationship you have with yourself, especially around trust. How can you ever go for your life goals if you don't trust yourself?

It's not going to happen.

One of my favorite practices is creating a list of things I know I can do, but that I'm not doing.

You might start with one thing. If you are reliable, maybe you start with a few more.

The whole idea is to start saying you are going to do something and then do it. Start proving to yourself that you are reliable, that you do follow through, that you can trust yourself.

There have been times in my life or with clients where it feels like nothing works. It feels like rock bottom, constant failure or disappointment. We aren't getting results, and nothing is changing or shifting. This can get discouraging. Sometimes when we get down like that we start to give up or give in to failure.

Often a great way to break this up is do things that you know you can already do but do them because you said so. For instance, do 1, 2, or 5 pushups right when you wake up because you said you would do a form of exercise and now you stuck to your word. If we do things we can do, win small games, we remind ourselves that we can and that builds trust in ourselves overtime.

You likely aren't at that level, however, building trust requires day in and day out practice.

A place to start might be to just notice where you aren't trusting and start practicing trust in that specific area.

For instance, I didn't have faith in my ability to stick to a reliable eating plan. So, I took on the simple practice of declaring that I wouldn't eat fries or ice cream for one week. I know it sounds like no big deal, but for me every time I eat out, I want fries and ice cream. Always.

So, one week was a baby step, something I could simply create some confidence around. Then it became two weeks and so on. And maybe for you it's one day or one hour, it doesn't matter, just make sure you can win at this game.

Set yourself up to win at this.

Sometimes we need a little win to give us that bit of confidence to start moving forward.

What practices can you take on that will support you in rebuilding trust within yourself?

FAITH

I want to end this chapter by talking about Faith. I define Faith as the active process to trust in others and in God.

I believe that all trust in ourselves stems from our willingness to trust in something larger. You need to get clear on your relationship to a higher power. You need to be clear on what you believe in, and whether these are beliefs are from your heart, or beliefs that have been imprinted onto you by your family or society.

Faith came in three stages for me.

Stage One was "Hard Work." When I was younger, because I

did not believe in anything else, I had to believe I could do it all myself. I had to generate all of my life and all of my successes. It even was hard to ask for help as I didn't trust or have faith in others.

Stage Two was "Magical Thinking." As I started building a spiritual connection, I shifted my trust to God and The Universe for the first time in my life. And because of this, a part of me expected things to happen magically. Many people will stop at their version of Stage Two, because it feels good and empowered. However, it doesn't take into consideration that you need to be in action to reach your goals.

Which brought upon Stage Three, "Co-Creation". I trusted myself. I had faith that God had my back. With these two beliefs, I was able to take action towards the results I wanted in an entirely new way. The world began to open up for me.

I remember the exact moment. I was in the shower, thinking about the challenges and obstacles that were currently in my way. Things weren't going well in my coaching practice, and they weren't going well in my relationship. I was afraid.

I was afraid that I couldn't make it as a coach. I wasn't good enough, no one would ever pay me what I wanted. I was doomed to fail. I was afraid and heartbroken that my relationship was crumbling. I was scared of being alone. But most of all, I was fucking terrified that if I gave up on this path, I'd revert back to being that asshole I once was.

As I stood there, I looked up and asked for help. I actually started to cry. I saw in that moment the heaviness that was upon me. I was feeling stuck. It felt like I couldn't handle anymore. But I still had faith, I choose in that moment to believe that I wasn't in it alone. That I had not only other humans but something larger that was with me. Choosing faith in that moment I knew I could actually handle anything.

There have only been a few moments in my life that I actually could feel God with me. This moment was one of them. The water in the shower started to warm up on its own, and I had the sensation that I was being held. I'm not going to even try to explain it, but I felt that something bigger had my back.

Having faith doesn't mean giving up and surrendering doesn't mean it will get done or created for you. It means choosing to trust without evidence and stand firmly in the knowing that everything will work out, and if you stay the course you will get, become, and achieve all that you ever wanted.

One of my favorite quotes is from a dear friend, Robbi Mermel. At one point when I was struggling, she said to me, "Trust in the faith of no evidence."

To me this means trust in choosing to have faith even though there is no evidence available.

YOUR TURN:

1) Decide to trust one new person. Just give them your trust without attachment to how, or what they will do with it. Give it away as a gift. See how it goes.

2) Get 100% clear on where your beliefs about God came from. What do you choose to believe?

3) What do you have faith in? Choose two new areas of your life where you would like to empower or embrace faith. Start practicing.

4) Bring faith and trust into all that you do. Trust and have faith in your abilities and choices.

20 | BRICK WALLS

◆ ◆ ◆

"All the adversity I've had in my life, all my troubles and obstacles, have strengthened me... You may not realize it when it happens, but a kick in the teeth may be the best thing in the world for you."

- WALT DISNEY

Bottom line. *I got 99 circumstances, and a chapter that hones in on obstacles that come with personal development. This chapter is about:*
- *Understanding that challenges are a normal part of our journey*
- *Identifying the most common obstacles that can arise*
- *Separating expectation from intention, in service of not quitting on goals*

CIRCUMSTANCES

"Obstacles don't have to stop you. If you run into a wall, don't turn around and give up. Figure out how to climb it, go through it, or work around it."

- MICHAEL JORDAN

W ho are you when obstacles arise?

Who are you when circumstances assault your plans?

Who are you when things get really, *really* hard?

I assert that your answers to these questions are the key to why you might not be where you want to be. Circumstance is one of my favorite subjects. Clients bring me all of their circumstances all of the time. And let's be real, sometimes, I bring circumstances to my coach too.

What I love the most about circumstances is that they always exist.

"Life is circumstances."

- ALEX TERRANOVA

Yes, I quoted myself and seriously, life is circumstances.

Let's make a list of just some of them:

The bus is late.

The weather isn't good.

I just got cheated on.

Someone is sick, or dying, or got hurt.

There isn't enough time.

I am too busy.

I can't afford it.

My partner just broke up with me.

My boss gave me too much extra work.

I just got fired.

My pet is sick.

My bank…

School is starting.

Summer is starting.

We are going on vacation.

I just had a baby.

We are remodeling.

My family won't support that.

I just moved.

I don't have a car.

Traffic.

My bike got a flat tire.

The dentist only had one slot open for me.

I have church.

I have kids.

My friend said…

My spouse...

My kids...

My house...

You don't understand...

We could probably write a whole book about the various circumstances we experience in life.
The point is that circumstances will always exist. They are normal. I point them out because the people who accomplish their goals, who create the lives that they want, are not run by their circumstances.

They are run by their commitments.

We have become a society that accepts people's circumstances, excuses, and reasons as acceptable and we are feeding into our own mediocrity.

We are brilliant. We are creative. We are creators who are dreaming new dreams and coming up with new ideas. Most of us are simply stopped by the challenges, or even just the thought of the challenges, that might come up.

Think about how much time we spend worrying about something that might happen in the future. It's crazy that all that time and energy could have gone into creating or achieving something in the present, now.

When I meet with a new client and they tell me what they want to create in their life, their big goals, often what comes next is all the reasons they can't or all the reasons why it might not be possible. And through the lens of most people we accept these, reasons, excuses, and circumstances. We believe and relate to them as true.

This doesn't work for me. If we accept reasons, we live a reasonable life. If you're reading this, I know you aren't interested in living a reasonable life. If you want to create your dreams and accomplish your goals you will have to be unreasonable and that will demand that you don't stop or buy into circumstances, reasons, and excuses.

When someone tells us they are late because of something we accept it. When someone tells us they didn't do what they said they would do because their child got sick we feel for them and we accept it. When someone tells us they didn't do whatever because they are just so busy it's okay, we understand. How many of us use the "I'm so busy" all the time…and guess what, we are all fucking busy. I don't know anyone who isn't busy.

> *"Being busy does not always mean real work. The object of all work is production or accomplishment and to either of these ends there must be forethought, system, planning, intelligence, and honest purpose, as well as perspiration. Seeming to do is not doing."*
>
> - THOMAS A. EDISON

I assert that the number one brick wall, or obstacle, that we as people must overcome in order to create the lives we crave is our relationship to circumstances. Succeeding requires living despite our circumstances, rather than living based on them.

COMMITMENTS

Earlier in this book, we practiced naming your highest commitments. If you didn't already, go even higher with them. For example, if you say your highest commitment is to your child, to money, to being in shape, and to being happy, we could say you are committed to Family, Stability, Well-

Being, and Joy.

Reach for the highest representation of the commitment, not just the details of it.

Have them? Great.

Think about your life. Are you focused on your commitments? Do your commitments determine how you run and operate in life? Do you stay focused on your goals? Do you spend time each day to move you closer to your goals?

Let's create an example:

Let's say I claim that I am committed to Family, Love, Well-Being, and Joy. However, I wake up late and miss my work out regularly. I work long hours that require me to miss out on family gatherings. I am too tired to spend time with my partner, or I distract myself with social media. Based on this life style, what am I actually committed to?

I may say Family, Love, Well-Being, and Joy, but looking at that life, it seems more like I am committed to sleeping, being late, working, and social media.

Our actions are one way to look at what we are currently committed to versus what we say we are committed to.

How does this tie into circumstances? Well, consider that there are circumstances that are entirely predictable for you. They may look like childcare issues, difficulty waking up in the morning, having a shitty boss, moving a lot for work.

Which circumstances most predictably have you act outside of your highest commitments? Or said another way, what circumstances occur that lead to you doing things that go against what you are committed to.

For instance, you're committed to wellbeing, but whenever

you wake up early in the morning to work out your child also wakes up and throws a temper tantrum, so you go to tend to your child and don't work out.

Knowing this, how could you plan or get ahead of those predictable circumstances?

OBSTACLES YOU ARE LIKELY TO ENCOUNTER

"Impostor Syndrome"

Have you ever heard of "Impostor Syndrome?" It's a real thing and it doesn't only apply to crappy con men.

How many of you have thought at some point or another that you weren't qualified or good enough for something you were doing or wanted to do? Maybe you felt like you were going to be found out. Or maybe you felt that you didn't actually deserve to be in the position you were in.

"Impostor Syndrome" or The Impostor Phenomenon was first described in the seventies by psychologists Suzanne Imes, PhD and Pauline Rose Clance, PhD. They describe that it occurs among high achievers who are not able to internalize and accept the success they have created.

These people often believe that their success and accomplishments are either lucky rather than a result of their ability, and they fear that at some point they will be found out by others and exposed as a fraud.

A study by the International Journal of Behavior Science in 2011 showed that 70% of people feel this way.

70% !!!!!

Other studies have shown that most CEO's biggest fear is that they are incompetent.

"Impostor Syndrome" is real and it's an obstacle.

Do you notice impostor like traits in yourself? While some people still achieve high levels of success with "Impostor Syndrome," most of us will not. And those that will often suffer self-doubt and will miss the joy of the experience of that success. Most of us would be stopped dead in our tracks at the idea that we don't know how, that we aren't deserving and that we can't: and if we try everyone is going to see how fucked up, stupid and terrible we really are.

So, what do you do if you see these traits in yourself? First, start noticing the voice in your head which keeps telling you about it. Get really practiced at noticing the fraudulent or untrue story that is bouncing around in your space. The more you notice it, the easier it becomes, and you will start to notice it as soon as it comes into your mind. After a few days add in a second layer.

Upon noticing it, make sure you tell yourself it isn't true, it's not real, it's just made up.
Another thing you might want to create is a Win and Accomplishment Journal. Write all your wins for the day, every day in the journal.

Wins can include:
Any accomplishments you had that day
Any compliments you received from others
Anything that stands as evidence of how capable, brilliant, and deserving you are
Anytime you notice imposter thoughts
Anytime you have or feel a sense of accomplishment

Leaving Your Comfort Zone

"Move out of your comfort zone. You can only grow if you are willing to feel awkward and uncomfortable when you try something new."

- BRIAN TRACY

Everything you want, that you do not already have, is outside of your comfort zone!

#Fact

I say that powerfully because if the things you wanted were in your comfort zone, you would already have them.

You either don't want them, or they are outside of your comfort zone. And since we already have talked about what you want, we know it's the latter.

I wanted to have a deeper spiritual connection. I wanted to be healthier and I wanted to be less insecure about how I looked. I created a practice of going to yoga multiple times a week and meditating daily. Guess what? It was uncomfortable.

I couldn't meditate. My mind would run on and on and on. The whole time I felt like I was doing it wrong, that I suck, that something had to be wrong with me. When I went to yoga, I felt terrible about how I looked in the eyes of all the in-shape yoga girls that were taking the class. I couldn't do the postures, I wasn't flexible, and I definitely wasn't wearing Lululemon.

What I wanted was outside of my comfort zone, so it required me to get uncomfortable, to not know how or what I was doing and to put down all the self-consciousness.

I didn't like it for a while. It took several weeks to build consistency, and there are still times years later that I struggle with it, but overall, I have grown to love yoga and meditation. They are the bubble bath for my soul.

Nothing makes me feel better than completing a hot yoga class. Every single time it pushes me in some way, shape or form, mentally or physically out of my comfort zone, and when I'm willing to lean into that space, I discover gold. I learn so much about myself and what I'm capable of. I often have some of my best ideas during the most challenging yoga classes. I believe my mind gets quiet enough to let my most creative thoughts rise to the surface.

With mediation, I gained mindfulness. My thoughts operate more slowly now. I'm able to choose my responses versus react to situations, people and circumstances. I'm more present and I'm more able to notice my thoughts and how they might not be on my side. Because I'm more able to hear The Hater, The Wimp and The Cheerleader the less control they have over me.

All of this required me to get uncomfortable. Think about anything challenging you've ever faced. That first time you rode a bike, or the first time you asked someone out. None of those things, or almost anything else you've ever did for the first time, was easy. They were outside your comfort zone often just because they were new or different.

So again, everything you want is outside of your comfort zone. Are you willing to get uncomfortable and create the life you want?

Setbacks

"How many people are completely successful in every department of life? Not one. The most successful people are

the ones who learn from their mistakes and turn their failures into opportunities."

- ZIG ZIGLAR

Setbacks are going to happen. They happen to all of us.

Nothing goes exactly according to plan. We might think we have it figured out. We might have planned for all contingencies. We might have worked all the angles. But regardless of what we do, how much planning we prep for, life is unpredictable.

If we live in a world where we simply accept that setbacks will happen, what can we do to get the desired results? How can we accept that things won't go as planned?

First, we must be okay with the fact that life is unpredictable and full of setbacks, challenges, and unforeseen obstacles.

We find out that we didn't get the job, or the person we are with isn't the right match, or we learn that the store we ordered all our new products from screwed up the order...

Regardless, if we want to achieve our goals we must keep moving forward when setbacks happen.

When a client fires you...

When you get dumped by the person you thought you were going to marry...

When you get fired or don't get the promotion...

When you find out someone else got the patent before you...

You must decide who you will be in the face of the setbacks and challenges that show up.

What does that mean, who you will be? While we've discussed this before, let's practice it now.

We are accustomed to having things happen, then doing something in reaction to it. And the results we get are slightly predictable because our customary actions and reactions are predictable. But if we choose a new way of showing up, a new way of being, and we create actions from that new place, we can create a new and different result.

A setback happens. And then you get to decide who you will be about it.

For instance, as I wrote this book, I got feedback and notes on things that need to be improved, deleted or added. My automatic responses: get upset, discouraged, and then either delay working on it or get right to it. Regardless, I approached it from a disempowered place of I'm not good enough and I just have to get this done.

Now, I practice something different I get the feedback, I get to decide who I will be about it. I choose to be grateful that I have people who care about me and support me enough to give me feedback and notes. Then from grateful I choose what action or actions I will take. I choose to read the notes from the view point of making my book and writing better. I choose to work on my book from my commitment to sharing and supporting others in creating their most powerful lives.

You have the exact same opportunities. Who will you be when (insert obstacle here) happens? Then from that way of being, what will you do?

I know this is like role playing but there are predictable things that do happen like feedback, people saying no, and people quitting, etc.

How will you get supported and keep moving forward?

How will you pick yourself up off the ground when you've fallen off your bike for the fourth, eighth or thirty-eighth time, and try again?

Create that plan now. Write out who you will be and what you will do when you encounter setbacks. Who will help you? Who will you call that will support you? What will you practice? What will you tell yourself or remind yourself?

Other People

It's weird to think of other people as obstacles, but they can present themselves this way at times.

People will get in our way and when they do, it will be up to you do decide if you will give in to whatever they present or push past them to create your life in the face of their shenanigans.

Frankly, people are sometimes the toughest obstacles you may face. Many of them might be those who you least expected to be obstacles. The people that you thought would be your biggest supporters often turn out to be the ones that are not supportive or down right difficult.

I don't necessarily mean that your parents or friends will intentionally try and stop you. People often react to change from fear or things that stem from fear like concern, jealously or a lack of understanding; they might think they are protecting you. This can look like they don't support you or understand you or have confidence in you. It may even feel like they aren't on your side.

So how will you keep moving forward when you parents don't support the changes you're making or the goals you're working to attain?

How will you keep moving forward when your best friends tell you to join them at the bar or the mall when you want to be working on your goals, projects or building your empire?

How will you keep moving forward when the people you want to believe in you simply aren't there for you when you need them?

This is a big moment, when people you know, love and trust aren't supporting you the way you want, who will you be about it?

Will you be angry, sad, or push back? Will you approach them with love, compassion and kindness and still maintain trust and faith in your own path and process?

What about people you don't know? Some of them will be supportive, but others won't support you or be positive. Who will you be in those situations?

Take a few minutes to take note of those people in your life that you know will support you in your journey of growth or in the pursuit of your goals.

Take a few minutes to take note of those people in your life that might create challenges, possibly from lack of support, not believing in you, fear, doubt, jealously, being negative or anything else that isn't supportive.

How will you use those that are supportive?

What will you practice with those that are not supportive?

Delayed Results

"The two most powerful warriors are patience and time."

- LEO TOLSTOY

We all know how this goes.

We have a goal, we have a dream and a desire. Maybe we even have a plan. We start hustling, working hard, networking, making calls, telling people about our goals, and creating plans and taking action...and we get excited and motivated by what is possible. Maybe we even start to see the thing that we want becoming more and more possible with each and every action.

And then, the winds shift. It's inevitable at some point. We hit a few setbacks. Maybe we push through and keep going and then, at some point along the way, the results that we imagined don't come as quickly as we expected or wanted.

Maybe we are looking at others' success and judging ourselves for where we are, like it's a race and others are doing better. For some of us we push harder, do more work, get more focused, revamp, retool and just keep going. And for others we get discouraged, tired, resigned, lose momentum or even the desire to continue.

What I know for sure is that results don't always show up quickly or as exactly as we expect them to.

This is normal. The key is to not let the current status of the process kill the vision.

Imagine a young man who loves tomatoes and decides he wants to grow his own. He buys some tomato seeds. He's excited to be able to grow his own tomatoes and make his own pasta sauce. He looks forward to putting fresh tomatoes in salads and even try some new recipes.

After finding the very best spot in the garden, prepping the soil, planting the seeds, and watering them, he waits. It's not too long until a tomato sprout pops up out of the ground. When the boy comes to water the plant and sees a sprout emerging from the soil, he becomes very upset! Pissed off even.

Why? Because he was expecting a grown tomato plant, and this is only a sprout. Through frustration and anger, he stomps it out, killing the plant and ending the process.

What do you get from this story?

Well you might be getting that the boy is an idiot and doesn't know anything about gardening.

If that's what you are thinking, let's try another example: You decide you want to lose weight, you start a diet and start working out. A week or two, or three goes by and you weigh yourself, or maybe months pass, and you haven't achieved the results you expected or wanted. You get upset, you give up, you quit the diet, you feel hopeless, you take it as evidence that you can't lose weight.

Both these stories highlight exactly what so many of us do in life. We start a project. The results don't look exactly like what we envisioned, or they aren't happening quickly enough, so we stomp out the whole process.

We quit, we get angry, we sabotage ourselves or our plans. We forget that often in life the work we are doing is actually planting seeds, and for seeds to grow they need to be tended to with water, sunlight, care, patience, and time.

We cannot fully control how results unfold. We can however control and choose who we will be as we work through the process of manifesting the results we want.

How many of us are stomping out our goals before they have the opportunity to grow and flourish?

How many of us are quitting because the results aren't coming as quickly as we want?

For a short time, I was living with a friend in Steamboat Springs, Colorado. I wasn't a hiker; at the time I had probably been on only a few hikes and I didn't love them. But while in Colorado I was practicing saying yes to new things, new adventures, and experiences.

My friend, an experienced hiker, took me on what was roughly a twelve-mile hike in the mountains. Our goal was to get to a lake she had heard about but had never seen. A few hours in, we were ten thousand feet up, deep into the woods and we still hadn't reached the lake. While I was in good shape, the hike was wearing me down. Not knowing how much further this lake was also was making the hike more daunting and challenging.

Hours and miles into this hike, there was still no lake. We had no idea just how much distance was left to cover, and we still needed to consider the hike back. We also realized we had not brought as much water as we should have. I looked at my friend and asked how much further we would be willing to go towards this lake before giving up.

We had committed to the lake as our goal, and we were willing to reach that goal no matter how much longer it took, how tired or thirsty we were.

Within ten minutes or so, we came around a bend in the trail and this glorious lake lay before us.

As it turned out, the goal had been right around the corner even as we considered giving up.

We often will not know just how close or far we are from what we want, and life has this funny way of testing us when we are almost there. Consider what may be on the other side for you when you feel tested. Are you willing to lean even just a little bit further into your commitments?

Keep Going!

Don't Quit!

Your goals might not always show up exactly how you envisioned them, but if you stomp out the dream or turn back you will never create them.

The only reason people aren't living their dreams and reaching their goals is because they stop, quit or settle.

Keep Going!

Expectations and Intentions

"The expectations of life depend upon diligence; the mechanic that would perfect his work must first shape his tools."

- CONFUCIUS

When I was in my twenties, a few people I knew had this strong belief that expectations ruin everything. They would say that when we don't have expectations things go great because there is nothing to be disappointed about, but when we have expectations the actual experiences of life never live up to them.

I spent years agreeing with this theory.

I don't believe it to be true anymore.

There is a difference between intentions and expectations. Expectations are simply the way you expect something to go from a passive place. Meaning you hope it turns out that way, but you won't play a part in it going the way you want. An intention is how you want something to go and from a place of creation you are willing to contribute to making it come to fruition. Intentions require more responsibility from the stand point of the creator.

Let's look at how intentions serve us and empower us versus disempowering us.

I believe the key to intentions is in not being attached to the results and taking responsibility for the process.

For example, you have a goal to be married, so you're dating and trying to meet the right person. You meet someone that you're excited about, so you start building up all the expectations around who this person is, and what they are like. When you go on your date and they don't measure up, you leave discouraged. You may even start to wonder if you'll ever meet the right person.

In this situation, you are attached to the results, so much so that the results will impact your ability to move forward powerfully onto the next date. In this instance, your expectations are pretty disempowering. What if the person of your dreams crossed your path after this date, but you were so discouraged that you didn't even notice them?

If you were unattached to the expectation or the outcome, consider that you wouldn't take it so hard if a date flopped here or there, as you would get that it's part of the larger process.

Not being attached doesn't look like not caring or being resigned. It doesn't look like quitting or stopping.

Being unattached might look like this:

You go on a date, and the person isn't who you thought or maybe hoped they would be. You notice your disappointment, and you allow yourself to feel it. Then you put it down. You remind yourself of the goal. You ask yourself if there is something you could be doing differently to support you in getting to the goal. You allow the experience to support you in becoming clear on what you do, or don't, want in a partner.

Someone who is attached to the outcome, can't let go of how it went. They apply meaning to themselves about it, they change the goal, or totally alter their plans in the impact of the results.

"True detachment isn't a separation from life but the absolute freedom within your mind to explore living."

- RON W. RATHBUN

In further exploring ideas of non-attachment I came across this article by Tamara Lechner on detaching as access to living a happier life. Lechner points out,

"In order to acquire something, you have to relinquish your attachment to having it... True detachment allows for deep involvement-because of the lack of attachment to outcome. The trick is behaving like an Oscar award-winning actor playing a role; become fully emotionally immersed and recognize that you can step outside of the character and be objective. The emotions in that moment are just as real as your dreams, goals, and plans. The ability to recognize that you can step outside and reflect-to not attach who you are to any desired outcome-is what true detachment is about."

Lechner goes on to identify some great clues that you are attached.

She says,

"When you are attached to an object, a goal, a dream, or another person, there are feedings that tell you 'If I don't have that, I won't be whole.' There are feelings like: Anxiety, Fear, Anger, Jealousy, Hopelessness, Sadness, Disconnection, Pride, Vanity"

So how do we get to a place where we can want something very much and not become attached to it?

Now we've all heard the expression, it's not about the destination but about embracing the journey. While that might be easier said than done, it is also key to not getting attached.
Enjoy the ride and embrace the journey. When we get so focused on producing or experiencing a specific result, we lose focus on the present moment. Suddenly, all the reasons why we started fade away and the thing that we want to do, pursue or create has just become another obligation.

When we look at expectations through a lens of attachment, we can see how expectations become the weapon that murders your excitement. However, if we are able to become unattached to the expected result, we can have the experience we desire while doing the work, aka taking responsibility, to create the results.

When we approach things from this place, we enjoy the ride, the process, and the experience.

This gives us the opportunity to learn from how it goes, to feel joy, excitement and keep us in the here and now.

When we work from this place and achieve our goals, great. If not, then we can view it as a good experience. From there, an empowered place, we can go back to the drawing board and retool, refocus and start working towards the goal or expectation again.

Let's touch on a few practices using intentions as a positive, empowering tool.

Here is a simple one:

Set an intention for things you do every day. For example, if you go to the gym every day, set an intention for how long your workout will be. If you love yoga, set the intention to use the time to connect with yourself. Have a date coming up? Set the intention to be honest, authentic, and curious.

Practice setting intentions everywhere.

Another practice is to be mindful. Specifically, be mindful of how the voices you have around expectations are being used for or against you.

What is The Hater, The Wimp and The Cheerleader saying about you, or the situation? What story are they using as evidence to prove who you are or who you're not?

This is practicing mindfulness. Notice your thoughts and notice the meaning that gets made up or created in your head. When you notice you are making up stories about yourself, regardless of whether they seem real or not or true or not true, pause and reflect that these are just stories and not facts.

For example, we tell ourselves we suck, or that we were disrespected. Or maybe we are thinking we are weird, or we'll never be successful. These are stories or interpretations, because in actuality they don't exist in reality, they are simply perceptions of reality. Because what you consider disrespected or weird is an opinion not a fact.

When someone yells at us, we create the story we were disrespected, when in reality, we were spoken to in loud voice. When you think you are fat because you weigh 300 pounds, the person who weighs 500 looks at you like you are skinny.

Most of what is going on in our head are interpretations not facts. Noticing this helps us break away from the stories that we interpret as truth.

Expectations are not your enemy, but they can be if you let them dig their teeth into you and give them more power than simply being an expression of how you would like things to go.

YOUR TURN:

1) Who are you when obstacles arise? Identify who you are in the face of circumstances, or when things get really, *really* hard.

2) Create a Win and Accomplishment Journal. Put the structures in place to use it daily.

3) Pick something new to try, like I picked yoga and meditation. Have it be where you practice setting a goal, setting intentions, and moving forward regardless of what circumstances would have you quit.

4) Bring faith and trust into all that you do. Trust and have faith in your abilities and choices.

21 | ONENESS AKA RELATIONSHIPS

◆ ◆ ◆

"You and I are all as much continuous with the physical universe as a wave is continuous with the ocean."

- ALAN WATTS

Bottom line. *Like it or not, we are all connected. This chapter is about:*
- *Recognizing the relationship that we have with ourselves, each other, and everything else in our universe*
- *Taking responsibility for the change we wish to see in our lives*
- *Shifting our current relationships to everything else around us*
- *Understanding Spiritual Reciprocity*

WE ARE ONE

On August 7th, 2019, there were three mass shooting, unlabeled acts of domestic terrorism, racism, and hate in the United States.

Three separate incidents!

As I drove to record a podcast this morning, I thought about how lucky, blessed, fortunate, and happy I am. I thought about how well things are going for me. I thought about how my life is so abundant, my practice is thriving, my business booming. I thought about how my social life, family, and relationships are going well. I thought about how I love where I live and the people who surround me. I thought about how I love my podcast, the guests, and appreciate all who listen. I thought about how close I was to publishing this book. I was grateful and happy.

And then I was hit with a tidal wave of sadness. I thought about the kids at the border being taken away from their parents. The people who feel they aren't welcome because The President and others have told minorities "Go back where you came from." The black males who have been beaten by police. The victims of the over 250 mass shootings this year alone. And even sadness for those that carry out the shootings knowing how much inner pain and fear they must suffer with inside.

As I drove to the studio, I became so clear, so present to the simple concept that you and I are one. That my life cannot be extraordinary if my family, my city, my town, my state, my country are a mess. If they are a mess, my life is a mess, we are one and the same.

Imagine you are a totally healthy person; you have no issues. Then suddenly you find out you have a serious kidney issue.

You no longer can call yourself a healthy person. While the rest of your body is fine, your kidney is part of your overall health, it impacts other aspects of your being and it cannot be compartmentalized from the rest of you.

It's the same when it comes to being human. When one of us is suffering, we all suffer. When many of us are suffering it's more detrimental. Your problems are my problems and my problems are your problems.

And until we get that, until we get that I am you and you are me, we are in trouble.

RELATIONSHIP TO EVERYTHING

I *love* the idea that we are in relationship with everything in life. This in it's most basic form is Oneness.

We have to be in a relationship with everything. You can't play tennis alone, you need someone to return the ball. You can't even play basketball alone, you need the ball, net and often the backboard for a reaction.

You can't know light without darkness. There is no up without down or right without left. And surely you can't know happiness without knowing sadness. All things are connected. Which means you have a relationship with everything, and it means everything is connected, and we are all, in fact, small pieces making up a much larger complex puzzle.

You might think I've lost my mind!

But give it a minute. Be open to what might be a new idea. I'm not claiming this is the truth, just another perspective.

If you are so attached to the ideas you already have, then it's almost impossible to grow and expand yourself and your mind. I trust that because you are reading this you have an open mind or are willing to entertain new ideas.

Currently, you are in relationship with this book. You are in a relationship with the room or space you are in, with the air you breathe, with the beverage you might be sipping, with your chair or couch.

Those relationships vary. For instance, you might hate this book and be suffering to get to the end, that's your relationship to it. Maybe you love the room you're in, it's comfortable and cozy and you feel safe and secure. That is your relationship to the room.

Maybe you have asthma and breathing is challenging and while you need oxygen it's not something that comes without worry or fear. That is your relationship to oxygen, the air and breathing.

I think you get it.

You have a relationship to money, time, happiness, your friends, your house, your partner, the government, your weight, your style, the city you live in and the vacations you take. The only common denominator in your life, and your relationships, is you.

If you aren't happy, it's not everything else, it's you.

If you are suffering or never happy, it's not everything else, it's you.

You are in an ever-developing relationship with everything in your life.

For some of you this might sound silly, but I invite you to take it in without agreeing or disagreeing. Just let it sit and see what comes up for you.

Where are you currently sitting? I'm assuming you are sitting or maybe laying down. If you are standing, take a moment and find a place to sit.

Now notice. How comfortable is what you are sitting on? Are you enjoying it? Is it supportive? Will the seat be there when you want to sit again? How is the environment around you where you are sitting? What is the temperature? The noise levels? What else do you notice about it?

This example is simple, and even a little silly. But it demonstrates your relationship to where you are sitting, and what you are sitting on.

For me currently, I am sitting in a room on a chair that is somewhat comfortable, but not super supportive for my back. The chair is good enough, but not great. It will likely still be here when I get up and come back to it.

I would say my relationship to this chair is that it's reliable and it holds me up. I also know that I am pretty unattached to it. If for some reason I got up and came back to a different chair, I wouldn't be particularly upset. I also know this chair is replaceable and old, so I don't necessarily see a need to take good care of it.

It's just a chair, but as you can see, I have a relationship to it.

Now let's raise the level of the conversation to something that probably matters a lot more to you: money.

You have a relationship to money, regardless if you have a lot of it, none of it, or live perpetually at Burning Man, where it doesn't exist.

YOU CAN'T SPELL MONEY WITHOUT 'ONE'

I want to use money as an example because for many of us, money can be pretty confronting.

Money gets us all worked up, makes us express or share our opinions, our righteousness and often gets us pretty wacky.

I ask all of my clients what their relationship to money is. Often, they pause, they aren't sure what to say. Many of them don't get it.

The follow-up question I have is, "if you were in a romantic relationship with money, as if money was a real person, what does your relationship look like?"

The conversation from here gets interesting. Clients say things like:

I ignore it, until I need something.

I obsess about every little thing.

I watch all of its movements, where it comes and goes.

I'm jealous of others who have a better relationship to it than I do.

I get angry when I don't have it and I'm so afraid of losing it when I do.

I don't pay much attention to it until it shows up and then I throw it away without thinking much about it. Then I worry how I will get it to come back.

I always have as much as I need. It comes and goes pretty easily and consistently.

There's never enough.

I learned early on that it was evil and that it's the root of all the problems in the world and I wish it didn't exist.

It doesn't grow on trees, it's hard to acquire and it takes a lot of hard work to get a lot of it.

In those examples, can you hear the relationship dynamics that are at play?

My favorite part of this exercise is that we could replace money with almost anything and you can see how a person relates to the things or people in their lives.

Now let's look at how this money relationship affects us.

If a person has a relationship to money such that they never believe there is enough of it and they are afraid to lose it, how might we expect that person to be doing financially? Or, how might we expect that relationship to be going? Or does how they feel about it even line up with the reality of their situation?

Regardless of which question, the answer is likely it's not going well.

IT'S UP TO YOU

At this point in the book, if you've been following along, doing practices and making changes in your thoughts, behaviors and patterns, you have the ability to make some really big changes in your life.

Now consider the concept that we just presented, the idea that we are in relationships with everything in our lives. This is very important because regardless of how those relationships are going, we have the opportunity to change or shift them.

One of the things I hear most from my clients is that they want things to change in their lives and they look for other people or other situations to do the changing. I'm sure something like this sounds familiar:

"I would be happy if my husband would just
_____."

"I would be getting more sleep if my kids would just
_____."

"I would be happier if my boss just _____."

"My life would be so much better if I just had _____
money."

"If the government would just _____ I would
_____."

"I'd be _____ if my wife just _____."

These are examples of expecting others, our situations, or circumstances to change so we can live the lives we want.

Guess what?

That shit ain't gonna happen!

The earth isn't going to shift and move for you. Neither your boss, your kids, your parents, your partner, nor your government will just change into what you want.

It's up to you.

How does this tie back into oneness?

Well if it's up to everyone else to change you are viewing them as separate from you. You are holding them as wrong or broken or something that simply needs to adjust. But what if you held them as you. What if instead of looking at others you viewed them as yourself and looked at yourself as the person to whom you could show compassion, acceptance, or changed something about yourself?

What if you viewed everything as you? If you took that level of love to everything?

SHIFT THAT RELATIONSHIP

We've established that you are in a relationship with everything.

Regardless of which relationship in your life you want to change, it's up to you to do the work to see that change happen. It is not up to the other person.

It is *not* up to the other person.

Often my clients hear this and retort, "but that's impossible! How can I change my relationship with my mom/spouse/boss/etc. if they won't do anything differently?"

When I got into the coaching and transformation space, and I realized that one of the things I most wanted was to shift the relationship I had with my Dad.

I've mentioned my Dad in other chapters. He is great. He is an example of success being possible through hard work. He was super involved with my brother and me when we were kids. He always supported us and encouraged us to be our best, work hard, and be committed.

I've shared a lot of what is amazing about my Dad in this book. And, there still came a time where I really pushed back against him.

I can't fully articulate how that came to be, but what I know is it reached a point where my Dad and I had a relationship that was like two ships passing in the night. We loved each other, but we couldn't connect. When we tried, the conversations remained shallow or resulted in disagreement.

It was in my first leadership, training, and transformation program, that I realized that I am fully or 100% responsible for the relationship I had with my Dad. I had created it unintentionally, but ultimately, I had created it.

While my Dad could take responsibility for whatever was on his side, it was up to me to be fully responsible for what I had put into the relationship.

100% is important. We live in a paradigm where we think things like, "I am responsible for my half, and you are responsible for your half." In actuality, we are responsible for *all* of it. I believe it is a lie that we can't both be 100% responsible.

I went to my coach and shared with her what I wanted to create with my father. It was one of the first times I really cried, not only from sadness that the relationship had gone on this long as it did, but because I felt horrible for how I had behaved in the past. And the past is nowhere to hangout.

I decided I was going to change.

I travelled home to LA from New York for Thanksgiving. After getting settled in at my parents' house, I asked my Dad if I could take him to dinner. He was a little surprised. I told him I just wanted to talk and that we could go anywhere he wanted. This excited him. I didn't see my Dad excited too often. Already this was off to a pretty good start.

We sat down in a booth of a little pizza place in Santa Monica and ordered. As we waited for the food, I shared with him how I was reflecting on my life and our relationship. I shared how it was really becoming clear to me that our relationship was my responsibility, all of it.

He was shocked to say the least, but he also wanted to take some of the responsibility. While this was nice of him, I really wanted it to be clear that I could take full ownership of how it had gone. If he wanted to do the same, he could, but he didn't have to just because I did.

During our conversation, I really let it all out. I didn't hold back my thoughts, feelings or emotions. I shared from the heart and apologized. I told him what I wanted to create moving forward.

This wasn't a 'let's hangout in the past' conversation. This was an 'I'm sorry for what happened, this is what I can own about how it went, and this is what I see for us moving forward' conversation.

It was a powerful moment in our relationship.

While our relationship is still growing and expanding, it couldn't have started to shift without that moment. Taking responsibility and declaring the future set the whole process in motion.

You might be thinking, why would you take all of the responsibility?

Well, first off, because you're a fucking grown up! And this is your life.

Whose life is it?

Yours.

If that's not enough of a reason, here's a little more. I believe we are either making our lives happen or we are victims of life and things happen to us.

Like you are either a piece of drift wood getting tossed in the current of the river or the salmon that swims up stream against the current going where it pleases.

From the 'we are making our lives happen' place, we take responsibility for all of it. All the choices, all the decisions, and everything we've done. This doesn't mean we take responsibility for the hurricane that took down our house, but we can take responsibility for who we are being about it after it happened.

From this place we have power. While each choice comes with reactions or consequences, we choose it. We don't get to just take responsibility for the good parts of our lives, we have to take responsibility for all of our lives.

In taking responsibility in my relationship with my Dad, I owned that I wasn't the best son, that I was disrespectful in all sorts of ways, that I didn't listen to him, hear him, show care and love and I surely didn't ever make an effort to connect with him.

Now let me jump forward a bit.

Since that time, I have continued to practice relating to my Dad from a different place. He has health issues, he's older and so I started practicing relating to him from a place of compassion and acceptance versus judgment, hostility and confrontation.

In short, I shifted who I was being with my Dad

I stopped needing to be right about everything. I didn't ask him to change anything and guess what, our relationship has shifted, continues to shift and continues to improve. He still is the same guy, he still believes in things I don't agree with, but that doesn't matter. I showed up differently and the results were different.

Sometimes I think about it like this:

Currently how I show up is equal to the value of 1. My Dad also shows up in a way equal to the value of 1.

When we come together, 1 + 1 = 2. Always.

The only thing I can change in this equation is myself. I can shift who I show up as, and in doing so shift my "number value" so to speak. Let's say to a value of 2.

2+1 = 3. The result is now different, even without my Dad changing at all.

This is how new results are created, simply by showing up differently. Practically, this might look like this:

I always show up as defensive and right, he always shows up as defensive and resigned, put our being together and we get the same result...no connection.

But if I show up compassionate, loving and open and he still shows up as defensive and resigned, we will have a different result. While I don't know what the result will be it has to be different.

But different is a step forward.

It sounds pretty simple. Is it? It depends if you are willing to be brave and courageous enough to take responsibility for your life.

Shifting how you show up in any situation will grant you access to a new result or possibility.
So, who are you being around money, at work, with friends and with your partners? You can shift those relationships if you are willing to practice being different.

What are some of the relationships you want to shift?

How will you practice showing up? Do you need to create structure to ensure that you practice showing up that way even when the other person or situation brings the same old stuff?

SPIRITUAL RECIPROCITY

I will close this chapter on oneness with a concept called Spiritual Reciprocity. It's something with which I have recently become familiar that pulls me powerfully forward and really supports me to see all of us connected in the bigger picture of the world.

In Psychology Today Larry Culliford says,

> *"Reciprocity means that if our intentions, speech and actions benefit even one other person, we too will reap benefit. Conversely, in the great scheme of things, if we intend, speak against, threaten or commit injury to another, harm will fall upon us and on those with whom we associate, our kin and kind."*

It's sort of a "what goes around, comes around" idea. But not from a magical place, from a realistic place; if we produce ills and harmful things in the world, we, by nature, will be harmed because we live in the world that we create.

Now when you look at your life, where are you not creating what you would want to come back to you?

Write down all the ways in which you are saying, doing or being something that doesn't line up with what you would want to occur for you. Here are some places to look:

Values

Beliefs

Mission

Purpose

Spiritual Beliefs

There is no secret sauce to shifting this, it's about looking at what's out and taking action to get it back in alignment.

What is currently out? What actions will you take to get back in?

YOUR TURN:

1) What are 3 areas of your life where you are currently unhappy with the relationships you have? Choose a new way of being to practice. Take note of what happens.

2) Notice when you look at others as separate from yourself. What situations do you find yourself thinking that it's their problem?

3) Who is someone for whom you haven't had compassion, love, generosity, or patience? Are you willing to apologize, forgive, and take responsibility for the relationship? Try it and see what happens. Warning: you must be brave and courageous to do this.

22 | LOVE

◆ ◆ ◆

"Darkness cannot drive out darkness: only light can do that. Hate cannot drive out hate: only love can do that."

- MARTIN LUTHER KING JR.

Bottom line. *This chapter is about love.*

Love is a feeling.
Love is a choice.
Love is an option.
Love is a sensation.
Love is crazy.
Love is abundant.
Love is scarce.
Love is fun.
Love is distracting.
Love is dangerous.
Love is magical.
Love is scary.
Love is tragedy.
Love is epic.
Love is unique.

Love is exhausting.
Love is freeing
Love is enchanting.
Love is heartbreaking.
Love is sadness.
Love is joy.
Love is catapulting.
Love is deserving.
Love is everything.
Love is nothing.
Love is godly.
Love is evil.
Love is dark.
Love is light.
Love is tears.
Love is smiles.
Love is peace.
Love is faith.
Love is suffering.
Love is happiness.

Love is everything and nothing. It is heart expanding and heartbreaking. But love is powerful and something we all desperately want, whether we are willing to admit it or not.

Your ability to love yourself has a direct correlation to the life you will live and how you will experience it.

Now you can hate yourself and live a financially successful life. However, if you don't love yourself, you will never actually appreciate your life, you will never be satisfied with your life and you will never be fulfilled in your life.

This chapter is intended to be short, because everything has been said about love a million times before I showed up here.

What I have to share with you about love is simple.

If you aren't willing to get your heart broken, you aren't open to sharing or receiving love.

Say what?

If you aren't open to the pain and hurt of heartbreak, you aren't open to the joys, intimacy and sensations of love.

This doesn't mean that you like heartbreak. Heartbreak can only occur if you actually love. And love can only actually occur if you are open to the inevitable possibility of heartbreak.

This really hit me when my coach explained it to me sorta like this, if you get a pet, you will likely fall in love with it. And with the love comes inevitable heartbreak, because one day, that pet will die or run away, and you will be left with a consequence of love.

While this might sound horrible, it's actually the miracle of love. If you didn't have the pain, hurt, sadness and all the things that come with heartbreak, the upside of love wouldn't be so miraculous.

It's like the pendulum of love can only swing as far to the right as it is able to swing to the left.

And that is the light and darkness of love.

So, love yourself and love others with such passion and unreasonableness that you get the experience of all of it, the ups and the downs. Don't short yourself any of the ride.

YOUR TURN:

1) Who have you been withholding or holding back love from? Willing to break that up? If you answered yes, go tell them you love them.

2) Notice where you aren't in a loving relationship with yourself. Practice relating to yourself as you relate to someone you love.

3) Have you fully processed the most recent heartbreak you encountered? If not, willing to do that? If so, go be with, feel, and honor the heartbreak. Feel it fully. Be with it. Let yourself experience the full spectrum of love and your humanity.

CONCLUSION

◆ ◆ ◆

"For me, becoming isn't about arriving somewhere or achieving a certain aim. I see it instead as forward motion, a means of evolving, a way to reach continuously toward a better self. The journey doesn't end."

- MICHELLE OBAMA

Anyone who goes through any sort of transformation at one point or another might come to see that there are two sides to themselves. There might be many sides, in fact but let's look at the prevailing two. These two sides can be defined in numerous ways: the light and the dark, the ways they were and the ways they want to be, the default and the conscious, the love and the fear.

For the sake of discussion, let's call the light, the conscious aspects we want more of and the dark, the subconscious aspects we are becoming aware of and likely want to diminish.

For most of us, when we start to see more of the light and become more aware of the dark, we want to kill off or hide our dark side. I sure did. I straight up referred to myself as "Bad Alex" and "Good Alex," like some wacky Dr. Jekyll and Mr. Hyde thing.

I believe we all want to be all light. And it makes sense. Even evil people who commit evil deeds often started with some idea about how what they were doing was good, or necessary or needed.

If you could kill and bury that part of yourself that was dark, that others didn't approve of or like, that you didn't approve of or like why would you not want to? If we could only be light, and love, and our greatness who wouldn't want that?

Have you ever heard of the concept of the divine dichotomy?

It's basically the idea that without darkness, there can't be light. Without evil, there can't be good. Without sickness there can't be health. That for anything to exist the polar opposite must also exist. How would we even recognize the one without the other?

We sometimes struggle with that as humans, as we just want one side without the other. But that wouldn't make sense. What would good food taste like if there was no such thing as bad food?

One of my biggest personal struggles is in embracing who my colleagues and I lovingly refer to as Douchey or Bad Alex.

As one of my mentors put it one day, "I bet douchey Alex is really fun. I bet he's great to go out with. And guess what, we all have a Douchey Alex inside of us. The important thing is to let that part of us out to play and not let it run us."

I know when I started changing my life, and adjusting my patterns and behaviors, I got hyper critical of myself. I needed to kill off the bad side. While I was never really a bad guy, I was run by ego, by lust, and I was willing to say and do things that hurt others so I would feel better about myself.

As I changed, I didn't want to wear the same clothes, I didn't know how to hang out with certain people. I didn't want to watch shows I used to watch or do anything that reminded me of "that guy" I used to be.

But it wasn't that simple. As a dear friend, who is also a brilliant Reiki practitioner put it, "you can't just lock that part of you in the closet and not listen to it. It wants to be heard."

I had to embrace my dark side. It was, and still is, hard, and continues to take tons of self-love, patience, and practice.

My dark side is strong, it's been practicing this way of being for over 30 years. My light side has been conscious to me for a fifth of that time. What I quickly realized was that I could bring them together and fully embrace how powerful, brilliant and creative I could be.

I know as a coach one of my greatest strengths is to be bold, to say the thing to my clients that they need to hear that nobody else will say to them. From my previous life, saying the bold thing used to hurt and offend people, so when I started embracing the light, I shied away from saying the bold thing. I was afraid of it. I realized that I could be bold from the heart and light and in service to my clients. It was one of the most powerful tools in my arsenal.

So, let's look back at the work we've done since you started reading this book.

What parts of you have you deemed bad, not good enough?

What parts of you have you decided you don't like or wished were different?

Now, if you're willing, take a deep breath and focus on one of the parts of yourself that you don't like, see as wrong, or bad.

Really focus on it and find a reason why you could be grateful for that part of yourself. Right now, be grateful for your inner workaholic, or for the people pleaser, or even the anger inside of you. Tell yourself you love it. Tell yourself that you accept it. Tell yourself that you forgive how hard you have been on yourself about it.

Actually say these things out loud now!

Love all of it. Every part of you is perfect the way it is, and you know how I know?

Because it cannot be any other way. There is no other reality in which it's different, it's just this, so it must be exactly how it's supposed to be, which makes it perfect.
And if you need more of a reason, it's hard to change things we haven't first accepted. It's also hard to change what we don't like about ourselves because it's like cutting out a part of who we are. It's like fighting against yourself. What we resist persists, so if you don't accept and love yourself or even your anger it's going to be hard to find peace and joy.

Creating self-love when you are in your dark place is going to be the anchor that supports you to get to your light, and to your goals. We need to embrace all of ourselves so we can do the work to grow and stretch ourselves.

The goal of bringing it all together is to start to integrate not only everything you've learned here but everything you've learned about yourself. Can you start integrating the dark and light sides of yourself?

HIRE A COACH

One of the best ways to start transforming yourself is to hire a coach. Why a coach? Because you can't coach yourself.

I'll say it again, you simply cannot coach yourself.

Did you know that roughly 95% of people believe they are self-aware and in reality, only about 10% are? That's a whole lot of people running around not having a clear picture of who they are, how they act, how their actions and behaviors aren't supporting who they want to be and the life they want to create.

Every professional athlete has a coach. High level CEO's have coaches. Presidents, actors and artists have coaches. They have coaches because they can't see their own blind spots.

We can't be objective, and we can't see ourselves from outside of ourselves. We don't know what we don't know. We can't see ourselves from any perspective other than our own.

A coach is there to reflect, to simply shine the light on patterns, behaviors and beliefs so you can step back and create some new awareness around them. A good coach won't, and can't, do any of the work for you. You must do the work, but a coach can help you identify what you are doing, and who you are being that isn't serving you.

Couldn't everyone use someone standing in their corner looking out for their best interests, pushing them to stretch themselves? Asking them questions to get them to reflect on life possibly in ways they never have before? Couldn't everyone use someone looking out for ways in which they self-sabotage and are holding themselves back?

If it's not clear at this point in the book here are a few more reasons:

- Coaching supports us to identify the gap between where we are and where we want to be
- Coaching pushes and stretches us more so than we would have on our own

Coaching provides support and accountability

- Coaching provides support and accountability
- Coaching creates a space to clearly and powerfully define S.M.A.R.T. Goals
- Coaching helps us see what's in our blind spots
- Coaching supports us to do and accomplish all those things we say we are going to do
- Coaching supports us to learn more about ourselves. To find out who we are and fall in love with ourselves

HOW TO HIRE A COACH

Okay, I want a coach!

Now how the hell do I hire a coach?

The first thing I would do is identify why you want one. A good coach will want to know where you are in life versus where you want to be. The reason for this is most coaches coach through projects. Projects are the things in our lives that we want to create, develop or accomplish, so they are our lives.

I usually want my clients to have three or four projects and usually I support them to create well-rounded projects, for instance a wellbeing project, a big goal, creative or dream project, a relationship project and maybe a money project. But really anything you want to transform or create can be a project.

Like I said before, nobody needs a coach. If you are fine, okay, doing good, making incremental growth, don't have interest in seeing what your full potential is you do not need a coach. And there is nothing wrong with that.

However, if you know you are capable of more. If you know you want things you don't currently have. If you know you have untapped potential inside of you and can't seem to tap into it. If you have a goal, a dream, an idea that you are hungry to create you might want to consider hiring a coach.

Now it's not my job to tell you what type of coach to hire, but what I would suggest is getting clear on what you want from your coach and what your goals are. After that I suggest contacting three coaches and requesting a sample session. Any serious coach worth their salt will gladly give a prospective client a sample session anywhere from 20-90 minutes so the client and coach can see if working together would be a good fit. Not every coach and client are a good fit for each other.

Some things to look for when trying to find a coach:

- Does the coach have a coach? If not, move on!
- Did the coach receive professional coach training? If not, I might move on.
- Do you connect with the coach?
- Do you believe or feel like the coach connects with you?
- Is the coach telling you or asking you things?
- Do you feel like you can trust the coach?
- Does the coach "get" you?
- Is the coach willing to be bold, and say things others won't normally say or reflect?
- How often does the coach work with you?
- Does the coach believe in the goals you are wanting to produce? Does the coach think they are possible?
- Is the coach willing to ask you questions that get you uncomfortable and out of your comfort zone?
- Has the coach worked with other people with similar goals? How did it go?
- Who does the coach like working with? What kinds of clients?

There are many more questions, but as I said, do three sessions and then choose. And remember there is no wrong choice so don't let that hold you up or stop you.

There is no way life is supposed to go, so you can't actually make a wrong choice.

WRAPPING UP

"I think the questions on the grit scale about not letting setback disappoint you, finishing what you begin, doing things with focus, I think that those are things I would aspire to or hope for all our children."

- ANGELA DUCKWORTH

There's something so cool about finishing something. Something so magical and powerful about doing complete work. Starting something, maybe getting stuck or stopped or challenged but eventually getting to the end and finishing it, perfectly or imperfectly.

I love that you are at the end of this book, finishing something you started.

Holy shit! I'm so present to the fact that I'm literally writing the final chapter of my first book.

Whoa!!!! That's a whole lot to process.

I've written a lot in my life, but I've never taken on anything as daunting as a book. And honestly, I didn't know if I could actually do it or not.

For a little over 10 years, I've wanted to write a book.

I put it off. I kicked the can. I ignored it. I distracted myself. I didn't have something to write about. I avoided and I did anything other than actually try and write it.

At some point, roughly 4 years ago I decided it was time. I

knew what I wanted to write about. I had ideas of how the book would lay out. What's funny is that it was the title, Fictional Authenticity...it came to me and I got inspired.
But inspiration runs out. So, I was left with a title and an idea and that's it. Months past and I recommitted to and generated an outline. Over the course of a month or so I flushed out the outline. A few more months past and all I had written was the introduction.

What was in the way?

The belief that I couldn't do it. That nobody would care to read what I wrote. That "who am I to think I can write a book" thought. All these silly, stupid made up stories got in my way and kept me safe and made it so I didn't have to fail.

At some point roughly a year after I wrote the outline I really started writing. I created the plan and about 7 months later I had written about one third of the first draft. And about two months later something clicked with the help of my coach. I identified some resistance around not being good enough, not knowing how to write a book, and the fears of being judged, I said fuck it!

I love writing. I love the way my fingers feel hitting the keyboard and watching the words roll out onto the page like waves rolling into the beach. I love feeling the divine power and connection of something larger than me flowing through me, through my fingers onto the page. I love the process and the journey and when I let myself go and stop caring about what others might or might not think, it seems like possibility opens up.

Then in two months, I wrote the rest of the book, which is two-thirds of the book in roughly one-third of the time. What I'm really present to is that it wasn't the process that was in the way. I could have forced myself to sit down and write, but what was in the way was the stories about who

I'm not or who I'm afraid to be.

I'm afraid to be great.

I'm afraid to have an impact.

I'm afraid to fuck shit up in this world and actually have it make a difference.

I'm writing this with tears in my eyes which is how I know what I'm saying is from somewhere deep inside of me. It's from a place bigger than any of us. It's a place that connects us all. This book isn't about me or my journey. It's about all of us and how we all are living Fictionally Authentic Lives that are stopping us, holding us back and keeping us from the divine greatness that is inherently in all of us.

We can all shed the layers of doubt, of myths or stories that have clouded who we are. We aren't bad or good. We aren't smart or stupid. We aren't tough or weak, or gay or straight. We aren't nerds or jocks or cool or lame. We aren't even young or old or fat or skinny.

Those might be things we are doing or spaces we are holding for ourselves in the moment, but we can change and shift everything, if we are willing. We have to want more for ourselves, our lives and for others than simply to make money, to have fun, to party, to be attractive, cool, or successful.

Don't we, at the root, just want to be joyful, feel fulfilled and satisfied with how we live our lives? Don't we all just want to be loved, give love and feel we had some sort of an impact while we were on this planet?

I don't know about you, but this book for me was my first real step into the light and out of the darkness. I've done so much work to get myself to the place that I could write this book from love, from imperfection, from not knowing how and knowing that nobody might even read it.

And getting here is where we find the gold.

Remember when you started to read this book, I told you who I thought I was. How all I wanted to be was a cool tattooed Zack Morris, slick, popular, social, and motivated by money and women.

Guess what, it's still there. That part of me didn't die. It doesn't even go away. I created that when I was a kid and frankly it's imprinted into my bones. But what I have learned and what I do know is that it isn't real, it's isn't bad, and that it doesn't have to have any power over me!

That's not actually who I am!

I created that and told myself that story so many times that the fiction became the reality, but it's not real. It's simply the myth that was my life. Every day I have to choose not to believe fiction that feels like fact. Every day I have to catch myself and notice where I'm coming from; is it my ego, my Hater, my Wimp, my Cheerleader or am I coming from love and heart and choosing my commitments each and every day?

Every day I have to let go of the past. I have to believe that just because it happened that way in the past doesn't means it has to happen that way in the future. Every day I have to forgive others. I have to forgive myself. Every day I have to remember that each and every day is a new opportunity, a new day to choose my life. A new day to make decisions and start creating again.

Yes, the past has led me to where I am. But today, I can do something new, something different and I can start showing up and being the person and living the life that I want and doing the things I'm committed to.

I'm not special. I'm just a guy. I'm not smarter than you. I'm not better looking than you. I'm not more charismatic or charming or funnier or richer than you. I'm also not dumber, uglier, weaker, or lazier than you. All those things are stories, they aren't real. They are just opinions, judgments, ideas, thoughts, and perspective, but not truth!

While we believe these stories and are under their spell, we can't live the lives we want. We aren't able to break the shackles and dive into the abundance that is life. Life wants us to succeed. God wants you to succeed. The Universe loves you and wants you to succeed.

Nothing is working against you, but you. Nothing is trying to stop you, but you. You, me and anyone can change and shift our lives but first we have to be willing to own and admit that the lives we've been living up to this point have been a lie. A lie called Fictional Authenticity.

If you want to end the lies, you first have to acknowledge that they are there and that they simply aren't true. So, we start there. We identify the stories. We catch ourselves living them. Then we start interrupting the patterns, the behaviors and the decisions the stories have us living. We can use this awareness to create a plan, a focused attack of commitment to get us to live the lives we want. To create the results we dream of. But mostly we can learn who we really are and fall in love with that person.

You can do anything you want, but if you don't love yourself it won't matter. At end of the day, if you don't love yourself, you'll never have enough money; you'll never be successful enough; you'll never be good looking enough or be dating or married to someone pretty, rich or kind enough, if you don't love yourself, it doesn't matter how great you are at anything. The space or container that is your heart will have a leak in it.

We do this work. We read these books. We write these books so we can take a baby step, one step closer to loving ourselves more.

What would you be capable of if you deeply and truly loved all of yourself? Not the self that is the story, but you, just you, without anything else. If you deeply and truly loved and cherished all of yourself what would you be doing? Who would you be spending you time with? Who would you be dating? What job would you have? How would you spend your days and where would you be living?

If we fully embraced and loved ourselves, we could do and be and accomplish anything and we won't ever be afraid to fail. Failure wouldn't even exist, as we would simply try again until we succeeded.

There are two ways to live life, one way is through fear, the other is through love. How are you living yours? Are you embracing life and expanding and growing through love? Or are you hiding, retreating back, staying safe and finding excuses in the circumstances and living through fear?

My wish for you in reading this book is that you found a little more love. That you treat yourself a little kinder. That you've started stripping off the layers of Fictional Authenticity.

My wish for you is that you embrace all your relationships from love. That you start going after what you really want. That you start waking up each and every day looking at your life through the lens of gratitude, love and compassion and start opening up with others and showing them your light.

My wish is that you put down the walls that you've built to keep you safe and start letting the love in.

My wish is that you get vulnerable and give others the space to open their hearts to vulnerability as well. I used to see vulnerability as a weakness, it was the space that enemies used to infiltrate or attack. But I know now that it's a strength; it's our greatest strength. Our ability to be vulnerable is the crack that the light shines in and out. It's the gap that allows love move into and out of our heart. The space that we give others to know it's okay not to be perfect, to have feelings, to get hurt, to be angry and to get back to joy. Vulnerability is the magic that let's my light connect with your light. It allows love and connection to move back and forth between us.

Go after what you want.

Live your life like you might not get another day.

Love hard, to your bones and don't be afraid to get hurt because that's exactly what makes great love possible.

Go after your dreams and don't be afraid to fall flat on your face, because anyone who has gone after their dreams fell flat on their face. At least once it's required, actually.

Choose everything everywhere. Choose the things you love and the challenges you faced.

Choose the best parts of your life and the worst. Choose everything to remind yourself that it's your life, it's 100% your responsibility to love it or change it. But it's yours.

Make everyday a day that you give and share love.

Make everyday a day that you take the time to find gratitude.

Show others compassion, you don't know what they might be going through and compassion helps ease suffering.

Practice being compassionate, rather than judgmental with yourself and others.

Take moments every day to focus on what you are committed to. Re-choose your commitments daily and keep working to be the person you want to be and create the things you dream of creating.

You are powerful.

You are divine.

You are vastly more brilliant, beautiful, powerful, creative, magical, divine, loving, forgiving, compassionate than you ever imagined.

Step out of your darkness and into your light.

You can do it...

Just keep going.

-Alex Terranova, DreamMason

Made in the
USA
Lexington, KY